RETHINKING WAVERLY

REDISCOVERING JESUS,
RE-IMAGINING THE WORLD | **JON ENSOR**

Rethinking Waverly:
Rediscovering Jesus, Re-Imagining the World
ISBN: 978-0-88144-178-9
Copyright © 2010 by Jon Ensor

Published by
Yorkshire Publishing
9731 East 54th Street
Tulsa, Ok 74146
www.yorkshirepublishing.com

Cover design by Hampton Creative

To Savannah, who makes me better

To Chris And Lisa for giving me the inspiration,
maybe I can return the favor

To my parents who started this whole thing

To Jovie for your patience,
and yes, now we can go on a walk

To Jeff and Josh for offering insight

To Andy and Ashley, who continue to inspire

To Tom for opening up a whole new world

To my many friends,
I hope this book does our journey justice

CONTENTS

RETHINKING WAVERLY

| INTRODUCTION

INTRODUCTION |

RETHINKING WAVERLY

I'm learning that things don't change because we see something new. Things change when we see the world in a new way. That's what is happening to me as I rediscover Jesus. That's this book. Since there is no formula for rediscovery, I think it's best I tell you a story.

I will never forget my first meeting with that pathetic excuse for a house that sat on Waverly Drive. My brother and his soon-to-be wife were in love, the sort of love that you only had to be in the presence of for a few minutes before you were happy without knowing why. Since their life was beginning, they needed a place of their own. The real estate agent showed them multiple houses in the city where we live. They had a few things they wanted. A fireplace was the clincher. After a month or so of searching, they announced that they had found the house and were eager to showcase it.

By the next day, our family loaded up to admire the house that had caught their eye. I wasn't sure what to expect, but as we turned into the neighborhood I had a good feeling. The streets were filled with updated cottage-style homes with steep-pitched roofs and manicured lawns. Through various turns we came to a street called Waverly. Then we finally saw … it.

I am pretty sure we couldn't see the house from the street. Weeds and other forms of plant life that have yet to be scientifically classified met us at the curb. The exterior itself was disappointing, but the interior was where it got ugly. There was an unfriendly smell that greeted us as we entered. The floors were a mess. The walls matched flawlessly. But, there was a fireplace.

We all stood there silently with that smile you have when you want to come off nice, but you know it's not working—the sort of smile you manufacture when you get a lame gift from someone you love. You know what I mean. But our apprehension was contrasted with their attitude. My brother and future sister-in-law stood there in defiance. They gave off a vibe that said, "What matters isn't what this place is but what it will be."

They spoke of the house as though all the renovations and improvements had already been made. They saw their home through the eyes of potential. Their love moved them to take this shanty-in-a-jungle of a house and make it something beautiful. I found the whole idea inspiring.

In the face of strange smells, deteriorating walls, and doubters, my brother and his fiancé found a fireplace and something called hope.

But this is not how we were taught to see the world. For many of us, our understanding of the world is similar to how I originally saw that shanty. We were told that this place is not our home. Not only was our world in ruins, but it was also unsalvageable. The only good news we heard was that we get to go somewhere better when we die, as long as we have our belief system nailed down. And if we were good, God would throw in some perks like health and wealth while we waited around. That's the world in which a lot of us grew up. Though I haven't gone anywhere, rediscovering Jesus has changed everything.

An old Englishman once told a tale of his journey to God.[1] He said he was like a young yachtsmen setting sail to find virgin lands to be claimed and explored. After watching the familiar shoreline disappear behind him, he set his face to the unknown. Days later, after confronting rough seas and sleepless nights, land was spotted. As the boat approached the shoreline, the sailor jumped out, flag in hand, ready to stake a claim to an undiscovered world. But just as the conquest was to be finalized, the young man realized he had miscalculated his route. He hadn't found any new land. In fact, he was back where he started. This was his country. This was his home. The man set off to discover something new and ended up finding something very old. Though he was back he started, the journey itself meant that he would always see that old world in a new way.

I am not that old Englishman, but I could be. I don't remember much of my early years, but parts of my early religious experience stand out. With clarity I can still hear phrases like, "If you died tonight, do you know where you'd go?" Eventually, I realized the morgue was not the right answer. My answer was supposed to be hell, and that was supposed to fill me with such dread that I made a few changes to ensure a better post-mortem destination. The question had its desired effect. I sat there, knees knocking, hoping the prayer took.[2]

But as I grew into a clear-minded, emotionally stable teenager, I began to suspect something was up. I wasn't sure why this group of people who warned me about the afterlife always wanted my money. I didn't understand why every Democrat was out to get me. I wasn't sure if every car crash or international conflict truly signaled the imminent end of the world. Even if this whole thing wasn't a racket, I wasn't sure that I cared. After all, I was a refined teenager. I had bigger issues, like wearing the right shirt and pretending I was athletic.

Somewhere during those years, I left. I walked away from the hell-fire sermons. I left behind the fear of being left behind. I ignored those guys who asked for my money. I stopped going to summer camp and getting saved. The only contact I had with that old world was calling a televangelist who asked me for $1,000, charged to my credit card. I asked him if I could still get the blessing he promised if I gave the money to my neighbor. He wasn't sure.[3] So like the yachtsmen I set out to find something better, something fresh.

Initially, I thought the place I discovered was new. But I too have come to realize I didn't go anywhere. I ended up where I started. I walked away from Christianity only to find myself a Christian. Though I've come home, I'll never see this world in the same way.

Like I said, I'm learning that things begin to change when we see the world in a new way. That is what Jesus continues to do to my understanding of him, myself, and the world. If it's okay, I'd like to share how rediscovering Jesus has moved me to rethink everything. It should only be a three-hour tour.[4]

Tonight, my brother and sister-in-law are blocks away, sitting in their repaired and remodeled home, enjoying each others' company and the presence of a warm fire. After months of hard work, their alternate vision became a reality. Their shanty is now a home. It stands out on Waverly as one of the nicest homes on the block. It would have been easy to pass on the house or easy to have it condemned. But my brother and sister-in-law's love moved them to rethink what was possible. I find God inviting us to do the very same thing with him and his world.

THE MEDIUM IS
THE MESSAGE

CHAPTER 1

CHAPTER 1 |

THE MEDIUM IS
THE MESSAGE[5]

My eighth year was my toughest. Things were great until I realized my teacher was a jerk. I'm not sure why people who dislike kids get involved in education. Someone needs to devise a filtering mechanism to get individuals like her out of teaching programs. She was the wife of a preacher, and I guess she felt education was her lot in life. A sort of Little-House-on-the-Prarie-worldview.

One day I asked her if I could use the restroom. Cheerfully, she declined. I asked again. Again I was shot down. As I felt a fire burning in my under-developed bladder, I wished I could fall into a seizure—anything that could get a lot of attention and sympathy and get it through her head that she needed to back off. That never happened, so I peed my pants. It was humiliating. My teacher didn't have much sympathy. My dad walked to my school to get me, meaning I had to walk home. It was a walk of shame. The event hung with me for a while.

Not long after that I found myself playing what seemed to be an enjoyable game on the playground. It was a variation of tag where two people were "it." Of course, this meant that kids were running for their lives in every direction. As one kid who was "it" locked onto me, the other locked onto my friend, Mike. Looking over our shoulders, we ran full speed into each other. I was a little taller. His forehead met my face. I woke up on the ground in a pool of blood. I was sure I was dead. After a few disorienting minutes, I realized that I wasn't on my way to paradise. Instead, I was on my way to the hospital with a broken face. It was traumatic. But it was only the beginning.

My face needed some reconstructing, so surgery was scheduled. I didn't think much of it. Imagining it was a sexier version of a doctor's visit with more candy when you leave and more time off school, I pranced off to the operating room. That was a big misunderstanding. I am not sure what went wrong, but I would also like to make a motion that we find some better anesthesiologists, too. Somewhere in the middle of the operation, on my face, I awoke. I am not sure the English language can put into words the terror a drugged-up eight-year-old experiences when he wakes up during his own facial operation. It was bad. Legend has it that it was on that operating table where I uttered my first curse word.

The trauma was so great that year that I decided I was done with school and doctors. I began faking exotic illnesses every Sunday night to avoid school, and I hyperventilated every time I had to go to the doctor. Though I'm unsure why, dentists became my mortal enemy. I think it was because they work around your face. Usually I would remain calm in the waiting room, but when it was time to go back to the office, I went nuclear. Hiding behind the dentist chair, I would be as threatening as a pre-adolescent could be, temporarily holding the head-rest hostage. There is an outside possibility I used some more bad words then, too. But as soon as the dentist gave up, I turned back into an angel and asked for my parting toy.

One time on our way home from another dental melt-down, my mom decided she had enough of my antics and expressed her disapproval. I am sure she felt like her son needed therapy, and she was probably right. I was upset at the feelings she shared, the surgery gone wrong, the existence of dentists, and my teacher who made me pee my pants. In protest, I threw my toy out the window of our car. I thought I proved my point. Like I said, it was a traumatic year.[6]

Trauma is interesting because it tends to traumatize. Meaning, it tends to skew a person's relationship with reality. The dentist was no real threat, and teachers are usually great people. But my experience shifted my perception. My perception became my reality.

BEATING A ROCK

There is a story in the Bible that connects with this idea. It involves Moses, a rod, a group of thirsty people, a rock, and a beating. In Numbers 20,[7] Moses' sister dies as the community of Israel settles in a region of southern Palestine called Kadesh. In what seems like no time, the community runs out of water. In their thirst-induced anger, they start a movement to overthrow Moses. So, Moses talks to God about the issue and then goes over to a rock, which he strikes with a rod. Water rushes out quenching everyone's thirst. Then, in what seems like a moment of divine crankiness, God tells Moses that he can no longer lead the nation of Israel.

It's a strange story. Is this God doing his best Zeus-like impersonation? Or did he just not get enough fiber in his diet? But like always, more is going on here. There are some important details that are often lost in translation.

The rock-beating occurred during a unique moment in history. The first verse says, "in the first month." It was the beginning of a new year. Actually it was the beginning of the forty-first year since Moses had led the Exodus. A generation earlier, Moses started a journey out of Egyptian oppression. The journey to the Promised Land should have taken a little more than a year. But because of some issues on the way, the journey went a bit longer. The story in Numbers opens not with those adults who left Egypt but with their children. Though Moses has led these people for forty frustrating years, this was a fresh start.

Geography gives texture to the story as well. The ex-slaves-now-nomads settled in a region called Kadesh, at the southern end of the Promised Land. The region had some history to it. This was the exact location where the ex-slaves rebelled against God forty years earlier. This was where the trouble began.

But the most important detail is Moses. He was a fascinating character. To sense the gravity of his role, think of George Washington, Mother Teresa, and Dr. Phil rolled into one. Moses was the figurehead of every aspect of society—political, spiritual, social. Since God cares deeply about such things, it meant Moses spoke exclusively for God. Moses was the medium. His actions were the message. If you wanted to know how God felt, you simply looked to Moses.

As Israel ended its forty-year sentence, Moses brought the community to a place loaded with bad memories. To add to those recollections, Moses lost his sister. Suddenly history started repeating itself as the people said, "Why did you bring us out of Egypt that we and our livestock should die here?" Same stuff their parents had said forty years ago. You can smell the trouble brewing.

As the trouble surfaced, Moses and Aaron went to the tent where God resided. There they inquired what to do about the growing coup. God told them to do three things.

Take the rod.

Gather the community.

Speak to the rock.

There is symbolic value here that is easily missed. The "rod" was also known as the "rod of God." This was the same staff that symbolically brought about the plagues in Egypt and other forms of divine judgment. I'm not sure if you were given spankings as a kid, but whatever was your mode of correction, you had that sinking feeling when the belt or "enforcer," as we called it, was revealed. That is the effect of the "rod."

But as the "rod" was displayed and the people gathered, Moses was told to simply speak to the rock. There was a message to be given. The people rebel, the rod comes out, and, right when you expect lightning bolts, there would be words and water. What would such a message communicate? What would this say about God?

Restraint.

Mercy.

Grace.

Kindness.

Hope.

After all, these kids never saw all the miracles back in Egypt. They grew up with poor examples of how to deal with difficulty. Now they were simply responding to sparse resources the only way they knew how. God wished to communicate his kindness in the face of complaining. Though it looked like history was repeating itself, God saw another possibility. He saw these misfits through the eyes of potential.

But this wasn't the message Moses communicated. Remember the three-fold message Moses was supposed to give? Well, here is what he actually did.

Took the staff.

Gathered the assembly.

Said, "Listen you rebels, must we bring water out of this rock?"

And hit the rock repeatedly.

Moses was to convey one message, but what picture of God did he actually share? Well, he called them "rebels." That is the same word that was used to describe the first generation that left Egypt but failed to follow God. It might sound today like, "You're just like your dad." All of the anger and topographic abuse painted a picture of a God who was angry, vengeful, and unsympathetic. This was a God who in his frustration had no hope for the current group of Israelites.

But that wasn't an accurate picture of God. That wasn't how God felt. That was how Moses felt. Moses was the one who was frustrated, weary, and hopeless. But Moses spoke for God. The God Moses illustrated was simply a larger, more lethal version of himself—which is why he found himself in trouble. Moses was the medium. His behavior was the only picture of God that the people were going to get.

The ache of losing his sister, the trauma of forty years of frustration, and the insanity of seeing it all happen again was enough to shape Moses' perspective. Perspective is reality. Sort of like when a dentist's office is held hostage by a traumatized eight-year-old.

REALITY

As difficult as it is for many of us to admit, perception is reality. It isn't that truth is relative. Sure, there are big objective truths. The problem is that there are only small subjective beings to interpret them. Just like in the account of Moses, there was something objective going on but Moses could only understand it through his own lens.

No one is truly an objective observer. We live in a world. That world has culture, language, and experiences. All those elements come together to form our lens. That lens becomes our mechanism for understanding God, ourselves, and our world.

If you're having trouble with this idea, think of your favorites. What is your favorite band, college, sports team, political party, or country? Why do you like those particular things and not others? It isn't as if divine revelation communicated to us that one band is better (whatever that means) than another. When we are honest, we realize our favorites have a lot to do with where we are from, how we were raised, and the many experiences we've had along the way. It isn't that our favorite college is better. It's that the brother we love attended that particular school. It isn't that our preferred political party has it all right, while the other is scheming to destroy the world. It's because we're from that part of the country or because our parents raised us that way.[8] We don't always choose our likes and dislikes. Often they choose us. We don't always shape our world. Our world often shapes us.

Like Moses, our perceptions are skewed. That might sound troubling but it shouldn't. If the biblical story is true, then it fits perfectly. We live in a world that has serious issues. It's a place full of hurt and wounds and bad third-grade teachers. Additionally, each of us is broken with our own destructive tendencies. Our experiences and our warped urges fill us with prejudices and complex motives. When all of that junk easily becomes our whole mechanism for understanding reality, what ends up happening? The same thing that happened to Moses. We imagine things are hopeless. We see things that are not there. We make God a larger, more lethal version of ourselves.

In 1851, a doctor from Louisiana named Samuel Cartwright published an article in a medical journal that described a new medical disorder. He called it "drapetomania." It was described as the desire to flee civilization. Cartwright observed this aspiration in African American slaves as they tried to escape their brutal white masters. Confused as to why any black man or woman would want to flee slavery, he concluded that it must be a psychological disorder. As he did what some loosely describe as research, he noted that drapetomania must be caused by the treatment of the slave owners. His research led him to determine that since slavery was condoned in the Bible, as in "slaves obey your masters," drapetomania occurred because slave owners failed to be biblical. But this isn't going where we think it is. He concluded that when slave owners treat their slaves as equals, this inflamed the disease. Instead, he said owners ought to dominate their slaves, preventing the onset of the disorder. He recommended that if a slave was showing any signs of dissatisfaction, the owner was to whip "the devil out of him,"[9] as preventative medicine.

We know this is absurd, don't we? How did Cartwright get so far off? Well, he grew up in a context where slavery was an accepted part of society. Cartwright was shaped to believe African Americans were sub-human and made by God for slave labor. He lived in a time where the idea of abolishing slavery meant economic collapse for his community. Both his culture and his experience allowed him to search the medical field and the Bible for something that simply was not there.

I hope no one reading this book is as caustic as Cartwright, but this sort of spin on reality happens to us every day. Recently, I read a newspaper article where a man in my state seriously damaged another man's reproductive organs simply because he was wearing the wrong team's shirt.[10] I also heard about a man who was stabbed to death in a parking lot because he apparently cut someone off in traffic. Both stories feature the bizarre, but they highlight what we do every day. We live in a broken world that adds to our broken perspective, which results in more broken things, even when we think we are right. It forces us to ask, how often is our perception slanted and faulty?

How many friendships have we lost because they didn't think like us?

How many harsh words have we spoken to defend an affinity that chose us?

How much time have we wasted convincing ourselves that our perception was gospel?

How many rocks were beaten because our past traumas colored our present moments?

PROJECTION

In the 1930s, a European politician said, "This man will set all of Europe ablaze with his incendiary dreams of world domination."[11] The statement fit the era well. But what borders on the insanely bizarre is the person who made the comment. Adolf Hitler directed the statement towards Winston Churchill.

Not only did Hitler have strong preferences and affinities, he also needed something external to excuse his actions. Like Cartwright, he saw something that wasn't there (a desire in Churchill to rule the world). But by placing his own intentions onto Churchill, he created an object to excuse his behavior. "If Churchill is going to try to rule the world, then we need to stop him" seemed to be the logic.

It isn't that we simply see things that are not there, we also feel the need to validate our position. We need to prove that our way is unquestionably correct. Think back to your list of favorites. Some of us genuinely prefer one thing to the next, but we also feel the urge to legitimize our perspective. Have you ever overheard an argument about sports teams or politics or religion? Usually each side comes to the discussion loaded with facts and statistics that prove beyond all doubt that their position is right. But did these people start out genuinely investigating the topic?

We know the answer because we do it all the time. We like our take on things, so we go looking for stories or authorities or 24-hour news channels that will validate our claims. The agenda needs support. Our perspective needs propping up. We work backwards. We start with the conclusion and then go looking for a premise. We start with an internal preference and then we look for external support.[12]

Psychologists call this a variation of projection. It can be defined as the "externalization of our internal feelings."[13] We want an authority to support our agenda, so we project our own biases onto that object to see the evidence we need. All sorts of externals, from statistics to studies to sacred texts to British Prime Ministers, are regularly rummaged through to find little gems that support our claims and wishes. It doesn't make us bad people. It is simply part of what it means to be human in a broken world. But if we have a tendency to use externals to back up our claims, what about the ultimate authority in our society? What about using God in the same way?

WHAT IS YOUR NAME?

Back before Moses had his rock-beating incident, he had an original encounter with God. There at a burning bush, God tells him about the plan to rescue the Israelites from Egypt and Moses' future role as liberator. Moses was taken aback by the message from the bush. Feeling the grip of his insecurities and fears, Moses questions God about the plan. The last question Moses asks is, "What is your name?"[14] God answers with the Hebrew phrase, *"Ehyeh Asher Ehyeh,"* which can be translated, "He who is" or "I will be there" or "I am that I am." Not exactly a concise answer. "Bob" would have done just fine.

But Moses was asking a question within a question. The popular thought in Egypt, where Moses was raised, insisted that knowing the true name of a deity meant that a person had magical powers of coercion over that god. So Moses was asking a question of reduction. He was interested in taking the God who talks through plant-life, who reverses oppression and turning him into a genie-in-a-bottle. The request was dangerous because inherently there was a desire to make God manageable. Moses was asked to embody God's wishes, the release of the oppressed. But Moses was asking God to embody his wishes. Moses was flirting with his own case of projection. The temptation was for Moses to take this God and use him for his own ends. But God's answer was brilliant. "I will be there." What is your name? How about a full sentence. It was sort of like God saying, "You aren't going to be able to figure me out, and you aren't going to be able to reduce me. I'm too big to be put in your back pocket, so don't try."[15]

Moses is an archetype for us all. We feel the pull to reduce God in some way. Our ancient ancestors called this phenomenon idolatry. It was a major problem because it was a step down a slippery slope. Idolatry comes from the Greek word *eidos,* meaning "essence, form, or perception." So an idol was a physical object that attempts to capture one's perception of God. This was understandable because people wanted to understand God. But what happened when God became captured in an idol is that suddenly God became well ... captured. God became manageable and malleable and small. Once God became small, he became whatever they wanted him to be. He became the supporter of the status quo, an insurance policy, and the sanctioner of unjust laws.[16] Eventually, this God ended up sharing all of their own perspectives. In the end, this "god" became them. This is what happened in most ancient religions. Like Isaiah said of all idol-makers and their creations, "He shapes it in the form of man."[17] The gods that were captured in idols ended up becoming the projection of peoples' desires. What started as a noble undertaking ended with the gods of money, sex, and power.

Most of us don't have idols lying around our house. Our temptation is the "idolatry of ideology."[18] Ideology comes from the same word *eidos.* It literally means ideas about the essence of reality. It is an attempt to capture the substance of God in an idea. Like our ancient cousins' struggle with idolatry, when God becomes limited to our ideology, God becomes manageable and malleable and small. Once God becomes small enough to be an idea, he can become whatever I want him to be. Eventually, this "god" ends up sharing all of my own perspectives. Essentially, he becomes a larger more lethal version of me. He can be a vengeful old man, a liberal, or a Republican. This is the story of our modern religion. What started with the good intentions of knowing about God ended in knowing about ourselves. We ended up with a God who agreed with all of our preferences. We ended up with a larger version of ourselves.[19]

Anne Lamott once wrote, "You can be fairly certain you have created God in your own image if it turns out that he hates all the same people you do." How often do you hear, "Well, this is how I feel about situation X, but I could be way off. I need to know how God feels about this."[20] When the god we worship ends up feeling exactly as we do about the world, we need to take a second look at who this god is. After all, God is meant to be reflected not projected.

STEWARDSHIP AND THE NEED FOR QUESTIONS

In the original creation story, God makes humans in his "image" and "likeness." These words carry the idea of reflectivity, meaning God has ideas and opinions of his own. The job of the human is not to take our preferences and stuff them down God's throat. Humanity's task is to grasp those divine ideas and implement them in tangible ways. The Bible is full of this notion. God says to Moses, "I have made you like God to Pharaoh."[21] That meant Moses spoke and acted on God's behalf. Paul writes, it is "as though God is making his appeal through us."[22] Being human is about being a reflection of God, because the world we live in is a reflection of us. In theology, our contemplation of God and his character and wishes is known as worship. Our implementation of his desires is known as service. The entire sacred task is called steward-ship—speaking and acting on behalf of a God that many perceive to be absent.[23]

To be fully human then is to realize what Moses didn't: that the medium is the message and that no matter how uncomfortable the compliment, we're the medium. Being human means we are speaking for God. If the medium is the message and we're the medium, then everything we do reflects the divine.

We are always speaking about God. If this is true, it means that we have to rethink our emphases. If you ask, "What does a Christian believe?" a person might respond, "A Christian is someone who believes in Jesus." This response usually means that a person believes that God exists and he has moved to forgive sins through Jesus. That's great and true. But if we are to take our image-bearing seri-ously, we have to move from simply having "faith in God" to having the "faith of God," from having "faith in Jesus" to having the "faith of Jesus." Changing a prepositional phrase might sound technical. But it means we have to be willing to move beyond faith as a litmus test for entrance, to faith as seeing the world from God's perspective.[24] Being a Christian is about having the humility and courage to ask, "How does God see this?"

But how can we ever manage to be proper mediums when we have a propensity for taking our arbitrary opinions and forging a god of assumption?

In one passage Paul writes, "We have the mind of Christ."[25] Apparently, a Christian is someone who has the ability to see everything from pollution to poverty through Jesus' eyes. It is a huge privilege and a massive responsibility.

In another passage, Paul encourages his friends to, "test everything."[26] Meaning, a follower of Jesus is actively engaged in the "mind of Christ" business. Having the faith of God is not a passive exercise where we assume God feels just like us. Instead, it is a journey of probing and thinking and praying.[27]

When we live in a world of projection and assumption, image-bearing is about testing. To have a good test, you need good questions. So image-bearing is about question-asking. Without questioning ourselves and our understandings, we will always fall back on a god who is a larger, more lethal version of ourselves. We will allow the trauma and tragedy around us to skew reality.

Some time ago, I watched a documentary about the space shuttle Columbia disaster. During lift-off, the shuttle was struck by a piece of insulating foam moving at over five hundred miles per hour. The scientists, who only had grainy video of the impact, determined there was nothing to worry about. What could foam do to a multi-million dollar piece of technology? They were terribly wrong.

The impact created a hole in the left wing, which made it impossible for the craft to journey back to earth. During the heat of re-entry, the shuttle broke apart and all seven crew members perished. In the months that followed the tragedy, officials discovered that the crew could have been saved if those in charge had done a few high-school level calculations regarding the weight and speed of the foam. Why didn't they? The investigation concluded that NASA slipped into working off of assumptions rather than inquiry.[28] Assumption led to tragedy. It usually does.

Questions can be unsettling. I think our aversion is connected to the inherent danger of a question. Unlike a static answer, you simply don't know where a question will lead. The fear of uncertainty and of being wrong keeps a lot of good people disengaged. But there isn't anything to fear with a genuine question. Questions are at the heart of being human.

Some time back, I was in a dusty airfield in the middle of Central America with my wife. As we were waiting for our plane to arrive, we sat next to a young boy who was busy talking to his mom. We don't speak Spanish well, but there was one repeated phrase that crossed the language barrier. *Por que?* Why? Most of us drove our parents crazy with the same word in our native tongue. There is something innate about us that longs to inquire. It comes from being made in God's image. Humans are wired to act on behalf of God, and in order to do that with any integrity, we need to ask questions.

Why?

Why are things the way they are?

Why don't we do something about this situation?

Why do those people have to sit at the back of the bus?

We came into the world with this sort of mentality. But somewhere along the way, we were told to stop asking questions.[29] Whether the message was intended or not, we were told that all of the understanding in the world had already been gained by the teacher, government, or preacher, and all we needed to do was sit up straight, be quiet, and listen. It is why most of us slept through church and school. It's called education by tranquilization.[30] And it works.

Without the art of the question, we would live in a primitive world. Inquiry is at the heart of progress. Someone had to invent something (a clay pot), and someone had to take that and make something else (a clay pot shaped like a dog), who made another something (greenery growing out of the pot), until we arrived at the Chia Pet. The whole process was started and sustained by questions like, "How can we make that ceramic dog have fur?"

A world without testing is a world without innovation, which is a world without Chia Pets—and that is a world without image-bearing.

Image-bearing as question-asking has other risks, too. There are individuals and institutions around us that do not want people to think new thoughts and see reality from another perspective. There are those in bureaucracies and even churches that use mindlessness and assumptions to operate.[31] Questions threaten to destabilize the way things are. Questions threaten to wake us from our slumber. When we begin to question and probe and pray, we become a threat to those who want control, those who want things to stay the way they are.

When we live by our gods of assumption, everything is settled and nailed down. Our temptation is to imagine we have God and the Bible and the world figured out. Like dissecting a cat in science class, we open God up, figure out where all the important stuff is, and then we are free to go to lunch. But after we have examined the cat, we can't expect it to get up and go play. So it is with our manmade gods. Such a god becomes so sliced and diced by our understandings and biases that we don't have to worry about this god doing anything unpredictable. When we do the hard work of "testing everything," we open ourselves to new possibilities. We open ourselves to a God who is unpredictable, who challenges our assumptions.

What started out as "why?" leads us to ask "what?" As in, "What does God want us to do about this?" "Why" always leads to "what," which leads to a lifetime of discovery. Ask a question like, "Why is there such an issue with poverty in one part of our town?" and follow it up with "What does God want us to do about it?" and you might just spend the rest of your life working out the answer.

Questions are not dishonorable.

Questions affirm the limits of our perspective.

They honor God by acknowledging that he has the best way of seeing the world.

They speak to our need to peer into the mind of God in order to carry out our task as image-bearers.

If you have answers to questions you weren't allowed to ask, then they aren't your answers; they are someone else's. You are being cheated. So are we.

CRAP DETECTORS

In the 1960s, an interviewer asked Ernest Hemingway about the characteristics of a great writer. Hemingway blew off the question. After a while, the interviewer begged, "Isn't there one essential ingredient that you can identify?" Finally Hemingway relented. "Yes, there is. In order to be a great writer a person must have a built-in, shockproof crap detector."[32]

In order to speak and act on behalf of a God who many consider absent, we too need built-in, shockproof crap detectors. We need to be able to smell distortion and assumption of all kinds, whether our own or our tribe's or our society's.

We live in a world filled with trauma and disappointment. With every terrorist attack or divorce, our understanding of the world can be skewed. It's tempting to allow our personal or collective shock to shape us and our faith. We're enticed to allow the pain we know to become the basis of a religion that confesses creation is bad, the point is going somewhere better, and while we're here our sole job is to live isolated from the mess of our world. In the shadows of the Holocaust and Third-World debt, we always feel tempted to divorce hope from history.[33]

But to be a follower of Jesus means we're the medium and the message is everything we do and say. It means that the world is watching to see a picture of a God that is something more than a larger, more lethal version of ourselves. As Chris Martin sings, "Reign of love, by the Church we're waiting."[34] The rest of the world is waiting to see something more than a movement that sums up all of our tragedy and trauma and disappointment with an offer for life after death and a decree to vote a certain way. It's time to leave the assumptions and clichés behind. It's time to see the world from another perspective. Because it's always about how we see the world.

Of course, the best place to begin asking questions is the beginning.

ORIGINS

CHAPTER 2

CHAPTER 2 |

ORIGINS

I'm convinced I started reading the Bible way too early. Much of the material made no sense, but it was interesting. Naked ladies who used the sun as a dress, monsters jumping out of the sea, people getting chopped up for no good reason, war, and famine.[35] It was strange but intriguing. Since I was told it was all true in a literal sense, the world became a very weird place.

At this point, someone usually says that my experience would have been better if there had been someone alongside who could explain all of this bizarre imagery. But there was.

There was nothing like another Sunday morning with the preacher talking about the imminent destruction of the world. I heard all about the coming plagues, God's anger, marks on one's forehead—you know, the standard story. I'm sure it got all the ten-year-olds on the edge of their seats. Then came the pitch. I didn't have to go through that mess involving flames and foreheads. I could pray this prayer and get off this God-forsaken place. I imagined it as a spiritual rocket ship ride to a better world. We would forget about the ugliness of this world as it went off into a certain lake. If I wasn't sure about praying that prayer, I would be given that timeless reminder, "You know this could be your last night."

I am pretty sure I cried the first twenty times I heard that message. Then it sunk in and became part of my view on things.

I lived on a nice street with kind people. I also knew about problems in the world. Without my early religious experience, I might have appreciated my life and cared more about the plight of others. But how can you appreciate the beauty of springtime while you are hoping to not be left behind? Or think of poor people in Africa when you're waiting to see a big naked lady dress herself in the sun?

This isn't about my disillusionment. This is about the reality that a lot of people who worship the risen Jesus are pretty excited about the idea of the world ending—and ending violently. It's not just the religious. Humans in general seem convinced this story of ours is going to end, and end badly.

How many made-for-TV movies depict the end of the planet?

The creative part of the story line is naming the culprit. Will it be an asteroid, volcano, pandemic, nuclear attack, earthquake, or tsunami? We even have some films where God gets the honor.

There seems to be a lust for a violent end to this world coursing through our veins. But that's because we have lost sight of the beginning.

SCOPES

Charles Darwin published his book *On the Origin of Species* in 1859. The book was a monumental move in biology, and jarring to society. In that era of history, the literal interpretation of the Bible was the authority. Darwin's ideas represented a challenge to that worldview.[36]

Tensions grew until the "Scopes Monkey Trial" of 1925. Until then, it was illegal to teach Darwin's ideas in the classroom. Those who disagreed with the law were looking for a fight. They found willing candidates in a backwoods Tennessee town wanting media exposure and a young biology teacher named John Scopes. Scopes wasn't actually sure if he had taught evolution, but it didn't matter. The town and Scopes wanted the spotlight. Both sides in the creation-evolution debate were happy to flex their muscles in moonshine country.

In what became a circus, both sides brought in their topflight experts. The verdict of the (ironically) seven-day trial was irrelevant. What emerged was the sentiment that to believe in a literal understanding of the biblical creation story was intellectually untenable. It was old world.

The respective camps left Tennessee determined to gain as much ammunition against the other and as many followers as well. The line in the sand was clear. Either you accepted modern science without question and left issues of faith to unstable humans, or you believed the Bible literally, developed pseudo-science to back up your claim and left the modern world behind, settling for easy answers to difficult questions.[37]

I can't help but wonder exactly how many hearts and minds have been sacrificed on that altar in the backwoods of Tennessee.

But the world isn't an "either-or" place. And those who paint reality as "either-or" usually have serious agendas they're peddling. The world is complex and intricate. To develop a healthy worldview, it is important to leave sterile "either-or" land and struggle to see an issue from as many perspectives as possible.

When you take a brilliant text like the creation poem in Genesis and stuff it into the Scopes Monkey Trial box, much of the wonder and rhythm is lost. That is tragic.[38]

ORIGINS

The origin story found in Genesis 1 wasn't written to give scientific proofs to a modern world.[39] It was never meant to be put on trial in the American legal system. It was told thousands of years before the trial ever took place. The origin story is actually a poem, and it circulated in a unique culture and unique time.

The ancient Near East was a complex world. As tribes and nations formed, each brought their own unique origin story to the table. Every tribe needed a backstory, something to shape them philosophically and politically.[40] The stories were designed to do two main things: offer a way of seeing the world and elevate a particular tribe or nation above its rivals.[41] One story, known as *"Enuma Elish,"* does this perfectly. It set Babylon up as the supreme race or tribe by describing the creation of the world and conquest of that creation by Marduk, who conveniently was also the chief deity of Babylon. Such a story gave legitimacy to the idea of conquest, domination, and empire. Origins matter.

The stories from the ancient Near East differ in many ways from each other. But there are some common threads that tie them each together.[42]

Often the world is created out of violence and promiscuity. One god murdering another god and using the corpse to make the physical universe seems to be a common template. Or maybe the gods cheat on each other, with the love-child being our world. There are variations. But over and over, the origin stories of the Near East speak to blood and lust standing behind the creation of our world. The world they knew was made by the hands of chaos.

Humans show up later in the stories. They are created as an afterthought or as slaves, so the gods could spend their time getting drunk. The gods' stance towards humanity is painted as tenuous. Humans were understood as a continual annoyance that needed to tread lightly. Habitual sacrifice to the gods was needed to prevent the latest famine or disease.

Since the god standing at the end of this whole creation process would usually be your god—the god of your family, tribe, or nation—it would have a profound effect on you. If chaos, violence, and lust were the tools that your god used to win dominion over the world, then how would that shape your understanding of reality?

How would that form your understanding of how to win in life?

In your business practices?

In your nation's foreign policy?

That is the point with origin stories. They quickly become controlling narratives. They become scripts. They shape our present and our future.

JONATHAN

A few years back I had a run-in with a good friend. We were playing soccer together, and he lost his nerve and went off on me. It was totally out of character for him.

After the game ended, I walked over to him to talk. In a matter of minutes he was discussing the real issue. His dad, whom he loved, had died a few years earlier from a drug overdose. His brothers, who are dear to him, were battling their own addictions and having legal troubles. We were close friends and I knew the details of his life. My friend wasn't simply upset because of what had happened in the past. He was afraid that it would happen again, to him. Since this was his story, he felt chained to his family's fate. My friend felt like his origin story was quickly becoming his destiny. He wanted no part of it.

We see issues like this all the time.

We are addicted to the same things our parents were.

We do the same kind of job our fathers did, just because that's what our "stock" does.

Our family has a history of divorce, and so we sense that is our fate as well.

How often does our past, our origin story, become our destiny?

As I listened to my friend in that parking lot, I realized he needed another story. It is something we all need. Often our narratives are filled with blood and lust, violence and abuse. Like my friend, we know that unless we get another story, we are going to play our role all too well.

Stories do more than put us to sleep at night. They shape us. They create our world, and, in a way, they create us. They mold our hopes. As a brilliant author says, "Stories create worlds; change a story and you change a world."[43] That is what the first chapter in Genesis is all about.

IN THE BEGINNING

In that same region of the world, another group of people, known as the Israelites, were told an origin story that was radically different.[44]

Genesis opens with the words, "In the beginning when God began to create the heavens and earth, the earth was a formless void and darkness covered the face of the deep, while the wind of God swept over the face of the waters."

Notice what is missing. There are no other gods. They aren't sitting around getting drunk trying to think of whom to seduce. There is no clash with other deities. No violence. No lust used to create. There is just one God and some sort of pre-created world.

The poet informs us that this world is "formless and void." One translator uses the phrase "wild and waste." The ancient Hebrew words are *"tohu va vohu."* Apparently, this pre-created world is empty and unproductive. The phrase can be understood simply as chaos. The world is barren. It's untamed.

The writer says, "The Spirit of God was hovering over the face of the waters." What is stunning here is God's interest in this chaotic world. The Hebrew word for "hover" carries the image of a mother bird watching over and caring for its young. In place of rivalry, violence or lust, we find commitment.   And like a bird caring for its young, it seems to be a commitment that this world become something more than it currently is.

Six creative periods begin with God saying, "Let there be." Each time God gets to creating, he makes a more complex and harmonious world. But this world isn't made out of nothing. This world is created out of *"tohu va vohu."* God takes the unproductive, barren, chaotic world and makes something beautiful and profound.

Like all other origin stories, this story would have a profound effect. The other stories were about the gods using violence and chaos as the means to create. According to those stories, to be on top of the world meant you had to have the tools of violence and lust at your disposal. But this story is about a God who sees chaos and waste and transforms it into something true and good. According to this new story, winning isn't about wielding brutality to get your way. Winning is about using creative energy to make life out of death and order out of chaos. No one had ever said that before. It was a huge jump down the road of human understanding.

But it doesn't stop there. The origin story culminates with humans created in the "image of God." This idea is mind-blowing in the ancient Near East. Only a king thought to be the "image" of a particular god. The idea was that a certain king would be ruling on behalf of a certain god. If you saw the king, you saw the god. If you heard the king, you heard the words of the god. The idea was a bit of a ploy. Ultimately it was about coercing a population to follow the commands of a tyrant with unflinching devotion.

But in this story all humans are created carefully in God's image. Even though this is one tribe's story, it isn't about the elevation of one race over others. This isn't propaganda used to prop up a king's every wish. Humans aren't slaves. They aren't an afterthought, and they aren't an annoyance. They are created to be the visible embodiment of the wise Creator. This is about the worth and vocation of every human no matter their gender, ethnicity or rank.

The first words given to these image-bearing humans involve a task. They are told to "fill the earth and subdue it" and "have dominion." Powerful words like "subdue" and "dominion" can excuse the existence of everything from puppy mills to strip mines. But that isn't what this passage is about. The Hebrew word for subdue is *kabas.* It means "to cultivate, to make better or develop." The phrase "have dominion" comes from the Hebrew word *rada* and it means "care-giving and nurturing."[45] Both words contain the idea of helping something reach its potential.

Here is the next development in this revolutionary story. If humans are to help the world reach its potential, then the creation of the world is ongoing, not static.

If humans are handed the task of making things better, then there is room for improvement. The world may be "good" but that doesn't mean complete. God started the task of creating but invites his image-bearers to continue the job.

Notice the last thing God does in this story. He rests. This isn't a case of divine burnout. This isn't so the gods can drink and laugh at the plight of humans, as in those other stories. God rests because he leaves the world in the hands of his image-bearers.

We know how that turned out.

WATERFALLS AND FRIENDS

Awhile back, I traveled to the only waterfall in my notoriously flat state. At the base of the waterfall was a warning for humans not to destroy the fragile ecosystem. Next to the sign was a used soft-drink bottle bobbing in the water. The message was clear; humans mess things up. There were no signs posted for squirrels to stand back or birds to watch their droppings. Humans had become a danger to creation. As I saw the bottle and the other trash that littered the area, I couldn't help but think, *Tohu va vohu.*

About a year ago, I received a call saying that one of my close friends had been in a car wreck and was not expected to make it. Weeks later we found out the crash was caused by a young man who made the decision to get behind the wheel after taking a mind-altering substance. Within a few minutes of reaching the hospital, we were told that she had died. She was such a beautiful person and had so much to offer. The tragedy was immense. Later that night, her mother invited her daughter's close friends back to the intensive care room. Words can't describe how tough that moment was. But as I stood there and saw my friend's body and all the people whose lives were shattered, the words were clear: *Tohu va vohu.*

I think the fiery prophet Jeremiah felt the same way. After reflecting on the materialism and exploitation present in his society, he says, "I looked on the earth, and behold it was formless and void."[46] These are the same words from Genesis. In some way, Jeremiah sensed what we feel all the time. The world that God made to be good and get better has plunged back into chaos. The humans who were given the task of making a more just world have failed.

Within this original and profound story is the idea that the world is pliable. It is bent and shaped by human hands. This means that even though humans are asked to further creation, they can also move her backwards.

Whether you are talking about fruit and a serpent, a trashed environment, or a destroyed life, it becomes apparent we have developed a talent for moving things the wrong way. The Bible calls it "the fall." With every step, we feel the ache deep in our bones. Thankfully, the story doesn't end with that ache.

HOPE

In a book called Exodus, there is an account of the empire of Egypt and their treatment of the Israelites. Apparently, the Egyptians have enjoyed hoarding the natural resources of the region for some time. With their accumulation of wealth, they now wish to build royal storehouses to support their economic and foreign policies. Not only do they like having stuff, they like having more stuff than necessary. So the only logical conclusion is to make more room for more stuff.[47] Since the Egyptians are formed by those other origin stories, that's just what they do.

Simultaneously, the ethnic Egyptians grow increasingly suspicious of foreigners, especially the Israelites who traveled there out of financial need.[48] The Egyptians reason they could take care of both problems with a single innovative program: build storehouses using Israelite labor. When empires dream up such progressive ideas, they always bring with them loads of oppression and brutality. The result is more chaos.

Exodus opens with this mounting storm. Just as the oppressive acts get ready to begin, the writer says, "But the Israelites were fruitful and multiplied."[49] The whole sentence seems out of place. It appears the author gets off track and seems interested in flaunting Hebrew reproductive capabilities. But more is in play here. The words "fruitful and multiplied" stretch all the way back to the Bible's origin story in Genesis. "Fruitful and multiply" was all about God's original idea for humans to actively participate in the furthering of creation. But here we are much further down the line, staring at the chaos and madness of an empire. And the writer has the audacity to insist God's plan for creation is unfolding anyway.

This isn't what we would expect to find on the eve of genocide, but there it is. Mysteriously and surprisingly, God hasn't given up on the world. It's as if the writer is saying, "It might look bad, but God's dream for this world and what it can be is still moving forward."

It is enticing to find a twisted form of justice in the idea of God doing away with this world and starting a new project light-years away. But the Scriptures begin with an account of a God who made the world and stands endlessly committed to its remaking. The world might have plunged back into chaos at the hands of humans who have deserted their post. But God is simply not willing to call it quits. This world is God's. It is precious to him. Even though we have messed things up, this is still his creation and he can't help but see the whole thing through the eyes of potential.

It is easy to be defined by mutating genes and genocide. It is easy to look at the people we have mistreated and been mistreated by and let that label our world. In the face of oil spills and outsourcing, it's easy to think God is no longer moving inside of history and is rather waiting for us to arrive elsewhere. It is easy to look at the pain and ugliness around us and let that become our controlling story. And from such a story it is easy for well-meaning people to invent a religion that is all about how this place is done for. But that is our story, not God's.

CF

I have good friends who early in their marriage were struck with tragedy. Months after their son's birth, he was diagnosed with cystic fibrosis. It is a terminal disease, which severely limits quality and length of life. Often, couples of CF kids don't stay together. The strain of sorting through it all is too much for many. But these two are making it. It's been incredible to watch. But what do they say to their son, much less themselves? How are they supposed to teach their boy to see the world? How are they supposed to keep cynicism and despair from destroying the whole family? How are they supposed to hold on to hope?

Exodus starts with slavery and possibility, genocide and promise, history and hope existing right next to one another. Maybe that is the point. Central to living in our broken world is finding the courage to believe in God's promise to make things right while dealing with our own Egypts. It is about life flowing with the hope that everything and everyone is going to be put back together again. It is about staring ridiculous injustice in the face and believing deep in our bones that this is not the last word on our world. It is about summoning the courage to believe that this place and everyone in it are destined not for dynamite but for a grand reversal.

As a good friend writes, "Glimpsing the way a story starts gives us hope for how it will end."[50] Though we groan at the chaos all around, our story is all about a God who sees something that is barren and unproductive and hovers over it all, just as he did in the beginning. He is hovering over my friends and their son. Hovering over the hearts broken by tragedy. Hovering over an environment that is groaning. God is watching, caring, whispering, "Somehow, some way, beauty is going to be made of this mess."

And when we discover the courage to hear that whisper in the midst of our own Egypts, we find the spine needed to re-imagine the future.

JESUS: COMING SOON

CHAPTER 3

CHAPTER 3 |
JESUS: COMING SOON

By the time a vacation is winding down, I am usually ready
to get home. At the risk of sounding like a travel brochure,
that was not my experience with Maui. Maybe it was the
weather. Maybe it was snorkeling with sea turtles. Or
maybe it was because my wife Savannah and I needed to
relax after putting so much time and energy into starting
our life together. It was our honeymoon after all. We
loved it and didn't want to leave.

One night as we were going to dinner, we came upon a
strange sight in the night sky. At first we could only see a
luminous haze against the black Pacific backdrop. But
after a few more minutes of driving, we saw a neon sign
that lit up the dark coastline like a lighthouse. The sign
read, "Jesus, Coming Soon," in large, brilliant, neon
lights. It sat perched atop a house that seemed fortunate
to support its weight.

As our time was ending in Hawaii, we thought we should
take a photo with the sign. After all, it was unique.
Making our way to the airport, we realized it was a
Sunday and we were going to have to make sure that we
didn't interrupt the open-air service. From a distance we
got out of our car to take the shot. As we positioned for
the picture, we noticed a lot of noise coming from within
the open air sanctuary. It was the morning's speaker. He

was yelling. About Jesus. About him showing up one day soon and about all of us leaving.

As I heard pieces of the familiar message, I was struck by how out of place "leaving" sounded against the backdrop of waves crashing, a cool morning breeze, and the warm tropical sun. Who, after all, wants to leave that?

THE END

Origins guide us. But our understanding of the end defines us. The way we think about the end matters. For a long time, humans have understood this principle and put it to use. The ancient Spartans had the odd practice of forcing their young men to envision a glorious death on the battlefield in the service of Sparta. This ancient form of brainwashing had a point. Starting people out with a vision of the end helped shape the Spartans into the ancient heat-seeking missiles they were.

We do this sort of thing all the time. Think about the art of the pep-talk. A football player is yelled at by some overzealous adult who is usually wearing spandex shorts that are two sizes too small. But beyond the fashion faux pas is the invitation for the player to use the vision of "winning it all" to give meaning to his tiresome workout. In some way, the future races to meet the athlete in the present.

We are shaped by our understanding of the future. Believing what "it" will be like gives humans rocket fuel for the present. Whether that energy is used to fight a battle or run an extra mile, it is always an energy that comes from the future and greets us in the present. In some unlikely way, the future ends up being about now. This idea is central to the writers of the Bible. When the Bible talks about the final chapter in the story, it always has one eye on what God is going to do in the future and another on what that means for today.

The study of where the world and the humans within it are going is called eschatology. *"Eschatos"* is the Greek word that means "end" and *"ology"* means "idea." Ideas about the end.

For much of the modern Church's collective conscience, the "end" is essentially about leaving. If you listen closely we receive these messages from everywhere. Our worship songs are loaded with escape. "God is bigger than the air I breathe, the world we'll leave," as a modern song goes. "One glad morning when this life is over, I'll fly away," says another older gospel song. Life on our planet seems to be actually about life on another planet. It isn't the most logical conclusion, but it's the paradigm most of us are working with.

This version of the end is huge because it turns our current world into little more than a gate at an airport, and death or making it to Jesus' return amounts to a boarding pass. Here and now amounts to sitting around a terminal, making sure our ticket is in order, doing our best to not do something analogous to yelling, "Bomb!"

If our aim is somewhere else, then the one place we can have no true lasting interest in is here. We may invest our money here, even in some good charitable stuff. We may treat a lot of the people well. But all of our investments in this place are tied up with the big payoff somewhere else. Essentially we become like one of those multi-billion dollar corporations that throws some pleasant parties and builds a few jungle-gyms for the city, all the while knowing that in a few months all the jobs are going overseas.

If we buy this version, then it's hard to stay attached to the here and now in any meaningful way. We easily become consumed with some other world, about going there, and about getting as many people as possible to journey with us. Once people are on board with the idea, the church's only function is to act as an escape pod ready for launch. Now boarding rows 15–30 ...

But is this how the early followers of Jesus saw the end?

Was the evacuation mindset that is so common to us well known to Jesus' original followers? Were they counting down the days until they left?[51] Was this life always about leaving?

PAROUSIA

There is a famous passage where Paul, the rabbi of the early church, encourages some friends who have suffered difficulty and loss and are sorting through their pain and grief. He writes to them:

> For the Lord himself will come down from heaven, with a loud command, with the voice of the archangel and with the trumpet of God, and the dead in Christ will rise first. After that, we who are still alive and are left will be caught up together with them in the clouds to meet the Lord in the air. And so we will be with the Lord forever. Therefore encourage each other with these words.[52]

When I was younger, there was a bumper sticker around my city that read, "In case of rapture, this vehicle will be unmanned." That sticker terrified me. I imagined those cars would become unguided missiles careening through parks and soccer fields. Ideas like the bumper sticker come from this very passage. The vision of the "rapture," a word that never appears in the Bible, has consumed the American church and tempted it to become a group of people waiting for the universal fire alarm to ring so they can evacuate. On the surface, that is exactly what this passage seems to be saying. But more is going on here.

Paul was writing to his friends in an ancient city called Thessalonica. The city was strategically located on a main Roman road called the Via Egnatia. At the same time, it was a port city. The location made the town very important to the Roman Empire. Early in its history, the city learned the fine art of the transaction. The more they kissed Caesar's backside, the more money and so-called freedom flowed into Thessalonica. It was a smart political move. But there was a catch. In the ancient world, politics, economics, and religion were intertwined. With the savvy politics came the religion of the empire, Caesar worship. The more they worshipped Caesar as "lord and savior," the wealthier the city became.

This was a bit of a problem for the early Christians, since they claimed Jesus as "lord and savior." To be a Christian in that city at that time would have been a threat to the economic stability of every citizen. The town flourished off of unswerving devotion to Caesar, and now a strange group of people not only no longer worshipped Caesar, but spoke openly of him as an imposter. When financial wellbeing is at stake, people can get ugly fast. That was life for the recipients of this passage. They were ostracized from friends and family, their businesses lost patronage, and their lives were threatened. The tension was thick. Throw in the deaths of a few of their fellow Christians, and you have some desperate people.

In the face of the mounting tensions, Paul says their hope lies in the reality that "the Lord will come." Again it sounds clear, but Paul is using a first-century nuance to make a dangerous and beautiful point. The Greek word for "come" is *parousia*. In the ancient world, emperors would often visit regions of their empire. The reasons were complex, but essentially the trip had two purposes. The king would show off his power and be worshipped by his citizens. But if the region was loyal like Thessalonica, the people hoped and expected the king would invest in the city. The investment would usually take the form of a building project or relief from a natural disaster. The image was clear. When Caesar showed up, things got better, situations were resolved. And his showing up was called none other than the *parousia.*

Same words.

Same idea.

Using dangerous political language, Paul says Jesus, not Caesar, will show up and things will get better. When he does it will be better than Caesar could imagine.

Paul writes, "[We] will be caught up together with them in the clouds to meet the Lord in the air."

Again, it sounds like God is going to steal us from the planet. So we need a little more history to come to the rescue. The English word "meet" is translated from the Greek word *apantesis.* When Caesar would journey to a certain city, that city would send out a delegation of citizens who represent the rest of the population. It is sort of like rolling out the welcome wagon at the airport for a friend or a foreign dignitary. That welcome wagon was known as the *apantesis.*

In the ancient world the *apantesis* was a collection of the most devoted citizens. It was filled with the kinds of people whose lives were centered around the king whether he was present or ruling from afar. These were the people who had given their lives to working for Caesar's agenda. As Caesar's entourage neared, they would leave the city and line the street waiting his arrival. When he finally arrived, Caesar would be joyfully greeted by the *apantesis,* and then he and the citizens would walk back into the city. That is how the *parousia* always went down. That's what the word always meant.

Paul isn't saying anything about leaving at all. There is nothing about people "going home" in death or disappearing one day. Instead he is challenging his friends to still have hope for this world. He is asking them to see Jesus as the world's true Lord, not Caesar. Paul is promising them a moment when this one true king will repair and renovate everything. Even death will meet its end as the "dead in Christ rise." This is comical since Caesar made his version of a better world through the threat of death, and Paul says Jesus will make his version of a better world by ending death altogether.

Perhaps the greatest stroke of brilliance is that Paul gives these people a job to do now. Life was tough. But they weren't victims, and they weren't sitting around waiting to be brought home. They were devoted followers of the world's true Lord. And since the real Caesar is coming here to this world, they were invited to be his *apantesis.* They were to be the people who worked for this anti-death campaign in anticipation of Jesus' arrival.

When Paul writes elsewhere, "our citizenship is in heaven,"[53] that doesn't mean the point is to go there. That's not how citizenship worked. The Roman Empire gave people citizenship not so that individuals would come back to Rome, but instead go out and set up mini-Romes throughout the world. They were to build smaller versions of the larger reality. If things went poorly, they didn't run back to Rome. They waited, trusting their lord Caesar would "come" and make things right. That's what Paul means when he writes, "And we eagerly await a Savior from there, the Lord Jesus Christ."[54] A Christian is someone who is setting up small versions of God's world. When things go bad we don't change our religion into a theology of escape; instead, we trust, we wait, we pray. Because we know God is coming here to make things right.

Actually, many of the words and concepts in the New Testament, such as lord, gospel, and *parousia,* originate from the Roman Empire. For instance, the word gospel was used to announce Caesar's accession to the throne or to commemorate his birthday. We need to be clear about this sort of thing. The Roman Empire was not out offering a gospel that provided for a warm, inner, spiritual glow that would eventually transfer into post-modern bliss. Gospel was an announcement that someone was running the show that could repair the world. When the first Christians followed the Gospel of Jesus, they were insisting the same thing. The Gospel is not salvation from the world. It's salvation for the world.[55]

For the first Christians, life was about bringing the reality of heaven to earth. They weren't delusional, thinking they could create utopia here and now. They knew the present wasn't going to eventually lead the future through hard work and innovation. Instead, they believed the future was going to crash into the present.[56] Jesus' empty tomb was the undeniable sign that the future was already on the move. As Jesus' followers, they sensed that the same force that raised Jesus back to life was now living in them. As their own souls healed, it forced them to look around and ask, "Where else can this happen?"

Their answer was "everywhere." When your rabbi comes back from the dead, you can't help but think there is hope for your marriage and your neighborhood.

Life was about shaping the world today, the way it will be eventually. It was revolutionary. It still is. Believing in the *parousia* of Jesus is to know that one day the future will break into the present and to sense that in mysterious ways, the conspiracy is already well underway.

BARACK OBAMA

I once asked a young friend of mine who was having trouble with this concept to tell me whom he respected and wished to meet. He said, "Barack Obama."[57] I said, "Fine, that works." I asked him what he would do if he was given an invitation to dine in The White House with the President. He said, "I would get a new haircut, a new suit, and I would learn some manners." That sounded about right to me. Then I asked, "What would you do if you found out plans had changed and Obama was coming to your house for dinner?" Startled he shot back, "Well, I would fix up the house, clean it up real nice, do some landscaping, and get my mom to cook something really good. And I would do all that other stuff I said before."

My young friend got it. When the idea is about showing up somewhere else, the focus tends to be on me, on getting my stuff together, on taking care of my own appearance and maybe bringing a few good friends along. That is how we were taught to see the end. But when someone shows up to our house, the center of attention is shifted beyond me, to everything I am associated with. That is the message at the heart of Jesus' return.

It wasn't a new thought to the early Christians. The prophet Isaiah said it brilliantly: "The glory of God will fill the earth as the waters cover the seas." It's a weird picture. Because of course the waters fill the sea. That is sort of the point of being the sea. But Isaiah is referring to the deep canyons of earth in which the sea sits. To him, it's as though the massive trenches were made to be filled by water. They are made for each other. That is the point. Just like the trenches and seas go together, so do God and this world. God will fill the earth like the waters fill the oceans, because God is made for this world just like the water is made for the sea.

God isn't just going to stop by for dinner. He is going to move in. This world is his house. It is a huge paradigm shift for most of us, but it has the power to change everything.

A NEW VISION ...

Let's play along with this perspective for a second. If God is coming here not to vacuum us up but to move in, how does that change things? If the healing love of Jesus is going to be unleashed on everything everywhere, what do you think that will look like? I mean, you picked up the book and chose to read this far, so you probably would enjoy a minute to hear your own thoughts. So, think. If this is true, then what will the world look like when this happens?

Will we have people living in luxury on one side of a city while on another the life expectancy is fourteen years less because of poverty?[58]

Will there be multi-million dollar church facilities to be used only by tithing members, when all of the pagan neighbors could use a safe place to play sports and have a meal?

Will people be objectified and dehumanized because of their appearance?

Will the school system in your hometown be completely unequal along ethnic and economic lines?

Will money be the thing that drives us?

Will status be our truest pursuit?

Will our addictions completely dominate us?

We know the answers don't we? When you place questions like these on the grid of God healing our earth, then some things that religion can make murky start clearing up. Often when we are told about the next phase of reality, we imagine a place full of bliss and absent of items such as economics, society, education, agriculture, and atmosphere. But if God is coming here, then everything here matters. Because everything here is going to be fixed.

So what will Jesus find when his *apantesis* meets him?

Will he find people who love the world like he does?

Will he find people who are as committed to it as he is?

Will he find people who have already jumped into the venture of being repaired and repairing?

Or will he find a group of people who have given up and are excited to leave?

Years ago, these questions came crashing into my mind in the middle of an evening devoted to "soul winning." It was a night when people in my church were to go out in the streets of our city "sharing the gospel." We had watched this sure-fire curriculum that was supposed to help a person see that they were sinners and were destined for hell unless they repented. It was no fun. But beyond it not being the least bit enjoyable, I began to wonder if it was totally wrong. Most of the people I talked to didn't seem too responsive. Some were even resentful that I would interrupt their evening to inform them of their status as a sinner. Imagine that. But I kept doing it because this, after all, was evangelism, and that is what serious Christians do.

But what if "sharing Jesus" is as simple as looking to the empty tomb and allowing the love that made it possible to transform ourselves, our relationships, and our city into something a little more like it will be when Jesus shows up?

What if evangelism wasn't about getting everybody to think just like me?

What if it isn't about getting everybody's bags packed?

What if it is about unpacking our luggage and investing in this place?

What if it is about us bringing a little bit of God's future to the present?

Maybe that would be all the convincing the world would need.

... OF GOD ...

This vision not only can change our understanding of the end, it can change our vision of God. The old evacuation theologies paint God as little more than a selfish, repressed, escape artist. The world is bad, so bad that it is beyond repair, so God is ready to get his people and go. It sounds like a little boy who takes his football with him when the game doesn't go his way. Instead of facing the issues around him, we're told God is going to make some alternate reality that is more to his suiting.

But the early Christians tell of a God who has hope for our present world. This isn't some naive or immature hope. This is a hope that grows from God's intention to confront the problems that plague our world. Instead of a God who is running away to another world, the God of the Scriptures is running into our pain and the mess we have made. This God takes responsibility for our issues. Here we find two rival visions of God: one who offers salvation by escape and one who offers salvation through repair.

A God who runs away and a God who runs into.

... AND OURSELVES

Not long ago, I had the chance to travel to Central America. One of the first things that hit me about the culture was the leisurely pace of life. People managed to work, eat, and enjoy family in a day and not once seem bent out of shape by traffic, long lines, or extended waits.

One of the first virtues you learn in many parts of the world like Central America is—wait for it—wait for it— patience. There is no such thing as fast food. Meals generally last hours. People get their work done, but it all happens at a much more modest tempo.

It is always great to get back home, but I can also instantly feel my blood pressure rising as I get back to American life. Horns are blaring in traffic. Everybody is rushing to get things done, with the hope of getting more things done (an interesting theory on life).[59]

I think our pace of life betrays something about us.

We are always running.

We easily find ourselves running after happiness, which we are tempted to believe lies in big money, big titles, and big respect from other insecure people like us. We want the promotion so we can buy the bigger house in the safer part of town that offers more creature comforts. To get that, we spend time running after the education and the spouse to go with it. In my own town, the general principle works off the idea that the more successful you are, the more you will gravitate to the southern part of the city, but the same thing happens everywhere.

McMansions and larger than life SUVs speak to our pursuit not only of happiness but of escape. We don't think of life in those terms, but it's true. We think we are pursuing happiness, but maybe we really are running from the problems we know exist. Please don't misunderstand me—our toys aren't bad, and an education is invaluable. But often we use them to get away from trouble that lies in one part of the city or the trouble that lies in our past or trouble brewing in our souls.

We feel the temptation to shop, dine, and live in the most updated parts of town and find ourselves not even considering the living conditions of those just miles away. The huge grocery stores, jobs, restaurants, and even churches come to our end of town so that we will never have to leave our haven and see the world beyond it. Sometimes, we even get theology on our side with messages that prosperity is ours because of some formula we've fulfilled, and those on the other side of town haven't jumped through the right theological hoops to attain the blessing of affluence.

When it comes to a culture where success equals flat-screen, it's all too easy to have life swallowed in the race after the technicolor dream. Every inch of life is eaten up by constant entertainment that brings with it bells and whistles and flashing lights. Again, this isn't a bad thing. But is it possible that we plug into something so we can unplug from the unpleasant realities of life?

A while back, I would see a friend of mine increasingly plugged into his MP3 player during every opportunity for social interaction. I later found out that the same phenomenon was happening at home. When we talked about it, he said it was his way of dealing with the pain and shame that was going on inside him. I think we can all empathize with that coping mechanism. We are tempted to detach. Our reflex is to run.

We stare at the TV so we don't have to face our failures of the day.

We stay at work to occupy our time so we don't have to deal with the issues at home.

We move to another part of the country because it will be better there.

We say what we did wasn't that bad.

We say it wasn't our fault and blame everyone else.

We indulge in denial, avoidance, repression, and playing the victim.

We are always running.

The truth is most of us have grown up with a Gospel that says that healing comes from leaving. Then we wonder why we tend to deal with the evil in the world and the evil in our souls by running away. But that isn't what we are made for.

In the aftermath of the racism, sexism, and violence that had seized his native South Africa, Desmond Tutu warned that "Unless we look the beast in the eye, we find it has an uncanny habit of returning to hold us hostage."[60] Running away does not fix anything. We were made in the image of a God who sees the pain and injustice in the world, calls it out for what it is, and runs into it, believing that repair is possible. If Jesus is the sort of God who is out looking for trouble and running towards it, shouldn't we try the same approach?

A Christian is someone who is looking for trouble.

We do this not because it sounds heroic or so we get on the evening news. Christians look for trouble in the world and in their souls because we believe that the future affects now. Similar to the Spartans and the crazed coach, we believe the future has a strange and powerful way of showing up to alter our present.

Even after that affair.

Even after those destructive years.

Even after that one thing that happened in our family that no one talks about.

Even though the issues in our city seem so big.

Even though the economy is in trouble.

RENTER'S MENTALITY

The first house I lived in was a rental. There were a lot of problems with it. Water came through the windows during storms. A fresh supply of splinters was available for anyone brave enough to walk barefoot on the floor. There were strange grasshopper-like creatures that roamed the house. But I didn't care. I was a renter, and I knew I was simply passing through. Better days of home ownership were just ahead. I am sure my neighbors appreciated my perspective. If things got bad enough, I could always wait for the contract to end and move.

No one wants to live next to renters. They aren't in it for the long haul. But take a renter and tell him the house is his, and everything changes. It isn't that the house now belongs to him and he can be the boss. Now he belongs to the house, and senses a responsibility to it. The tools come out. The floors are sanded. Because this is now something sacred. This is now a home.

For those of us who grew up with a spiritual renter's mentality, the *parousia* is sort of like someone handing us the keys to the very place we assumed we were passing through. It's about looking at the world and allowing this place to become our home.

It's an opportunity to re-imagine the future and rethink what we should do with our present.

Hopefully the tools will come out soon, and we'll get to work.

But before we do that, we need to rethink an essential tool. Many people use it as a weapon, but it is meant to be an instrument of healing.

It's time to rethink morality.

CROSSING LINES

CHAPTER 4

CHAPTER 4 |

CROSSING LINES

A while back, I went to my nephew's dedication. It was a meaningful evening. Everyone was excited. For one reason, we had a new person in the family whose drool and snot made us smile. Also, there was a profound sense that one day this little guy was going to do something great. We knew that this greatness was tied up in three things: God, the parents who were going to put all their love and energy into raising him, and the wider family that was going to spoil him rotten. So all of us together in a church sounded just about right.

After the dedication ritual, a guy stood up to share a few thoughts. He wanted to remind the parents of their responsibility to raise their children well. He gave them some pointers. He told parents to keep their kids away from pornography, to keep their kids away from drugs, to keep their kids away from bad friends, and to keep their kids away from conflict in the home. They sounded like good ideas to me. But that's where it ended. It was a list of what parents were not to do. The only thing they were told to do was to bring their child to church. Like I said, it was a great night, and a few thoughts from a well-intentioned guy, but I knew I had heard it all before.

"A Christian is someone who doesn't drink, swear, chew, or go with girls who do."

Most of us never sat through a course on morality, but we didn't have to. This proverb was our Cliff Notes version. We understood Christianity, like baby-dedication-guy, to be about not doing bad things or being with bad people. It often works as well as asking a diabetic to not think about sugar cookies. But is that all morality is?

Morality is defined as "a doctrine or system of moral conduct."[61] This might be the most unhelpful definition ever. Words like "doctrine" and "system" sound fixed and static. But that isn't the truth about morality at all. Lots of people have lots of ideas about how to live. Those ideas compete and change and grow. So maybe it is more helpful to understand morality as a dialogue. It is an ongoing discussion about the best way for humans to live. It is a discussion that charges much of our individual and corporate lives. Whether it's every four years or every minute on the 24-hour news channel, our whole civilization obsesses over morality. We may not think of it in such terms, but follow me for a minute ...

over here.
on this side of the conversation we have
sexual purity
family values
hard work and discipline
believing the right things
honesty
personal morals
an elephant
it's about being good

on this side we have
protecting the environment
helping the world's poor
educational reform
equality
social ethics
a donkey
it's about doing good[62]

The conversation is usually unproductive. Not because healthy dialogue is unneeded, but because most of the dialogue breaks down into an argument about how one side is right and the other is wrong. It's "us" versus "them." No one seems to know how we can find common ground. We were born into this polarization. Without our consent, we were brought into a world that forced us to choose a side and defend the cause—usually by cramming our friends' in-boxes full of propaganda about how the other side is initiating programs to murder puppies.

ROCK STAR

Not too long ago I was reading *Rolling Stone.* One article recorded an interview with an influential rock star. He is the antithesis of baby-dedication-guy. He is known for his good music and heart for social morality. In the interview, he discussed how he was brought up in a strict Catholic home with stringent rules for believing and behaving. He was raised by baby-dedication-guy. He spoke of how he had left all of that personal morality stuff by the wayside to pursue bigger things like justice and better trade practices.[63] So, he left the discussion about personal/sexual restraint and discretion to enter a discussion about international restraint and discretion? Yes. We know tons of stories that sound similar.

If we are honest, this sort of progression, if you want to call it that, doesn't sound consistent. You would think a person who sincerely opposed nations manipulating and objectifying each other would feel the same way about the opposite sex. You would think he could see the similarity between our personal urges and drives and those urges possessed by corporations and governments. But our culture doesn't allow it.

I think a lot of us identify with rock-star-activist-guy. We grew up with baby-dedication-guy and got so tired of simply being told to be good, that we flew to the other end of the spectrum looking for something there. But it's the same disease.

Both baby-dedication-guy and rock-star-activist-guy are suffering the symptoms of that unproductive conversation. It's an illness that prevents us from thinking and praying deeply about our world and our role within it. To protest the wave of international exploitation caused by economic urges and not understand the profound similarity to our own personal drives is a massive failure. To think that we have no responsibility for the betterment of the world other than abstaining from everything except "going to church" and "reading our Bible" is tragically immature. Both represent a failure of the most dangerous kind. It's a failure to grasp reality. It's a breakdown in understanding the human being and our impact on the wider world. It's a failure of perspective. It represents a false step down a steep descent filled with bombs, tears, and one night stands. When we can't see the terrain well, we need to move to higher ground.

FOLLOW GOD

In the Bible, Moses says, "It is the Lord your God you are to follow."[64]

Up to this point in history, following God was a literal experience. There was a visible pillar of fire that led the Israelites through the wilderness. But Moses gives this command as times are changing. Moses is about to die. The people are done walking through the wilderness. There will be no more fire or smoke, no visible manifestations of God. So the question is, "What is Moses getting at?"

The early rabbis discussed this extensively and came up with the idea that Moses was telling the people to imitate God. One rabbi said, "As he clothed the naked, do you clothe the naked; as he visited the sick, do you visit the sick; as he comforted mourners, so do you comfort those who mourn, as he buried the dead, so do you bury the dead."[65] Following God changed from literally moving from place to place to cultivating a character and lifestyle like his.

This way of thinking is fundamental to the Bible. Living a certain way was never supposed to be about earning points or getting into heaven. Living right is about becoming who God made us to be. Since we were made in his image, we are at our best when we are like him. Morality isn't about an elephant or a donkey. It isn't about an election. Morality is about becoming truly human.

If morality is about acting like God, then we have to ask, "How in the world does God behave?"

At the heart of Christianity is the beautiful conviction that when you see Jesus, you see God. If God seems too transcendent or too foggy, then simply look at the life of Jesus to clear things up.

CROSSING LINES

One of Jesus' most famous stories is known as the "Parable of the Sower."[66] The parable is about four different kinds of earth. Three kinds of soil do not sustain life, but one works well. Now there are a hundred different ways of interpreting this passage,[67] but at the heart of it is the message, "Some people will get it, and some people won't." Some will hear Jesus' retelling of the story and some will miss it.

The art of the parable is often missed. I've heard that Jesus' parables are "an earthly story with a heavenly meaning." But this ends up saying that Jesus is using physical objects here on this planet to help us understand another distant reality that we might see when we die. This was not a part of Jewish thinking. Instead, for Jesus, a parable was a teaching method that uses simple physical objects and processes to help people understand another way of seeing this world.[68]

In the "Parable of the Sower," Jesus compares himself to a farmer, and his life-altering way of seeing the world is symbolized by the seed and people as soil. Some will get it, some won't. Some people are shallow, some are hardened by life, some can't stand opposition from the dominant culture and sell out to the false gods of money and power. But when some people hear the message, things click; things change. These individuals are able to see life from another perspective, and they themselves seem like they are coming from another place. Their life has a productivity and vitality about it that changes things. But in Jesus' world, the major question would be, "Where is this good soil? Meaning, where are the people who get it?"[69]

There would also be some assumptions as to the answer to this question. A normal Jew would look out at the world and naturally assume that the good soil was Israel. After all, they were the ones who worked at keeping the Torah and loving God with a pure heart. They were the one who had cultivated a deep appreciation for strict personal morality. The "bad soils" would be understood as the dark pagan nations surrounding and occupying Israel and those Jews who were colluding with the occupying forces.

Most of us come from a very Hellenized understanding of education. I know you're smart, but I'll say it anyway: Hellenism refers to the influence that Greek thinking has on the Western world. Our schools and universities are structured in a way that reflects the influence of Socrates, Plato, and Aristotle. In this method of teaching, the goal is usually to learn something intellectually and then move on. But this was not the world of Jesus. Jewish teaching always understood that a person learns what he does.

So we think, "Great little story there, Jesus, now what are you off to do?" But for Jesus, the lesson is not done. Some will get it, some won't, and the question that still lingers is, "Where is the fertile soil?"

After a few similar parables, Jesus loads up his young Jewish disciples and heads across the lake. It might seem like Jesus is interested in an ancient sunset cruise, but he's not. It is a moment loaded with meaning.

When they get to the other side, they pull up to a cemetery where a screaming man in the buff runs to greet them. Jesus heals the man of his demonic possession and then throws the demons into a heard of pigs that throw themselves off a cliff.

It doesn't take much interest in historical context to appreciate that we aren't in Kansas anymore. If we're pulling up to a cemetery with naked men and pigs on a nearby hill, then this isn't Israel. Pigs were regarded as not only unclean but symbolic of the brokenness of the world. Similarly, cemeteries and those who made contact with the dead were untouchable. Jesus was taking his followers to another land. This was enemy territory. The other side of the lake was similar to our wrong side of the tracks. To get into a boat and go "there" was to journey to a place that is symbolic of everything that is wrong with the world.

But why does Jesus do this?

What point is he trying to make?

Twelve is a significant number in Judaism. God chose the nation of Israel to be a "kingdom of priests." They were to be a nation or kingdom. But not just any nation. Just like ancient priests, they were to reflect God. Their main export was to make the Creator God more accessible and understandable. They were to be a community of people who embodied the true nature of God for the rest of the world. This community was comprised of twelve separate tribes. But this project was facing some serious hurdles.

The books we call the Old Testament, also known as the Jewish Bible, record the tenuous relationship between Israel and God. The plan was for God and Israel to partner together to work towards undoing the mess humans had made of the world. But Israel couldn't hold up her end of the deal. Eventually, the whole nation was sent off to exile. It was the most troubling event that happened in Israel's history.

When Israel eventually returned from exile, the nation recommitted to getting things right. But their improved performance didn't result in a meaningful change to the current world order. The only logical conclusion that many of Jesus' contemporaries reached was that Israel was not doing a good enough job fulfilling their end of the contract. So they poured themselves into a hair-splitting effort[70] of understanding their obligations, so they could get things right.

But after all the hair-splitting, their vision of getting things right ended up with them living in an isolated contentious relationship with the rest of the world—the very world they were chosen by God to save. By the first century, Israel had become a community that lost a larger vision of its mission and instead obsessed over its own moral and racial superiority. "Being good" grew into "being better than." This was a massive problem to Jesus.[71]

When Jesus chose twelve men, he was referring back to the ancient idea about what it meant to be God's people. Jesus used their activities to be symbolic of what Israel was always supposed to be. It was an invitation to join his renewed version of God's community. So, Jesus loads up the twelve young men who came from a culture obsessed with "being good," goes to a place that they were "better than," and he makes things better.

Jesus was and is raising questions about the purpose of personal morals and the purpose of religion itself. He is calling into question his own community's misunderstandings about the interplay between the condition of our own souls and the condition of our neighbors' welfare. To miss the connection is to miss morality altogether.

This story isn't just about doing good things, helping people, and starting charities. To be Christian is to affirm that Jesus was sinless. He obviously cared deeply about his personal morals, but so did the rest of Jesus' world. Jesus points out the error of obsessing over personal morals while disregarding the "other side of the lake." He believed passionately in being good, but the journey across the lake is about the need to take our personal morality and do something with it. Being good is good, but only when it makes the world better.

Remember the question looming at the beginning? "Where is the good soil?" Well, in one sense, the good soil exists in people who have the courage to take their goodness across the lake, like Jesus. But as the account ends, we hear that the man Jesus helped is changed. He wants to go with Jesus. But Jesus tells him to go back to his own world and tell them what God is like. The man goes, and everyone from his hometown is "amazed."

Where is the place where God's life grows?

In the most unlikely places.[72]

But this kind of transformation only occurs when people who are good learn to be good for something. This kind of thing happens when people who are "good" begin to see the wrong side of tracks as "good soil." But that can only happen if we see the other side through the eyes of potential.

There's being good.

There's doing good.

And there's Jesus' way. Being good to be good for something.[73]

BABIES AND WIDOWS

The first five books of the Old Testament are called the Torah. Right in the middle of the Torah is a book called Leviticus.[74] It's a strange book for Westerners to read. But the goal of the book is to help humans recapture something they lost.

The beginning of the Bible speaks about God's original design in creation. In Genesis 1, there are the repeated phrases "separated" (as in light from dark and sky from the waters) and "each according to its kind" (as in God created differences between flowers and turtles and horses). Those words are meant to capture the symmetry and orderliness of God's original intent. But the entrance of sin into the world represented a distortion of that symmetry. In some way God's original design was threatened by the recklessness of sin. The road home to God's re-imagined world runs through a return to symmetry. That's the point of Leviticus.

Leviticus was designed to give those ancient Israelites a sense of how they could reorder their lives in a world overrun by chaos. It's a book about how humans are meant to live. That means it is a book about morality. Much of the content might look to us like legalistic rules, but it was meant to breathe purpose into human existence. Every aspect of the ancient Israelite community was structured with meaningful rituals and rhythms. Since God's original design was full of meaning, Israel functioned as a miniature example of what the world was always supposed to be like. Morality is finding something we've lost. Morality is about repair.

The version of morality found in Leviticus wouldn't fit our world well. There are rules and regulations for how humans are to interact with God (as in sacrifices and long lists of what not to do). But there are also as many rituals and expectations for how humans were to interact with each other. They were to be holy by not seducing their neighbor's wife, and also by taking responsibility for the poor and the immigrant.[75] There was no separation between sacred and secular. There was no room for making lines between personal morals and social justice.

When Israel lived out a balanced and symmetrical morality, it thrived as an example of how to live and became a medicine that made things better in the world. But when

Israel became asymmetrical with its morality by disregarding its own lifestyle or the welfare of others, it became toxic. The word in Leviticus for this out of balance life is *tuma*. It is often translated "unclean," but the word is closer to our concept of "radioactive" or "polluted."[76] When Israel's morals grew too small to include both God and people, the result was fallout. Fallout for Israel. Fallout for others.

Morality is always about the endless interplay between "us" and "them." On a long plane ride, I had the chance to talk to a good friend, who also happens to be an accomplished doctor. After catching up, he referenced the huge amounts of anti-depressants prescribed to successful people in our city. He said there were no local studies being conducted, but there didn't need to be. He and many of his colleagues noticed the same thing. This seems out of place, doesn't it? I live in a typical midwestern American city. On an average street, there are as many churches as chain restaurants. Faith and luxury live side by side. With a combination like that, how could so many people suffer from depression?

My expert friend had a theory. He said people are cut off. I wasn't sure what that meant so I asked him to explain. He simply said, "Garage door goes up, garage door goes down." My friend went on to speak about how modern people deal increasingly with the feelings of isolation. If you're too hot, you push a button. If you're too cold, same thing. If you want food, push another button. If your kid gets restless, sit them down so they can push more buttons. You can actually go for weeks without being outside for any significant amount of time or having a face-to-face conversation. The few times a week people do leave the house, they often sit down to a sermon that tells us how to be good and how to stay away from bad things. Just when the brilliance and creativity of many people could intersect with the suffering in the world, they hear about how bad the world is and how they are to keep those forces from entering their home. People full of life return home isolated from the other side of the lake, exiled from themselves, while they push buttons. It's asymmetrical living.

Like it says in James,

> Religion that God our Father accepts as pure and faultless is this: to look after orphans and widows in their distress and to keep oneself from being polluted by the world.[77]

The words used for "pure" and "faultless" are the Greek nouns *katharos* and *aspilos.* They are connected to the terms used in the Old Testament for sacrifices, as in, the animal sacrificed is to be pure and faultless. It's easy to think that sacrifices were just barbaric attempts to earn God's grace. But that wasn't the point. One word for sacrifice in Hebrew is *korban.* The phrase literally means "near bringing."[78] This is huge. The Bible starts with God and man living together. Then things get messed up and Heaven and Earth are divorced. *Korban* is about brief moments when God and man, Heaven and Earth are brought near. *Korban* is about healing and repair. Sacrifice is anti-fall. James is talking about sacrifices, but he is also talking about morality. For James, the true kind of *korban* that heals and repairs is not a certain animal, but humans that care both for the condition of their own souls and the amount of food in their neighbors' pantries. It heals us from our own button-pushing exile, and it brings more justice into the world.

True spirituality is about understanding that the only sort of morality that repairs is the kind that has enough room for our own inner health and the people around us who need our help. Being a follower of Jesus is not about entering into a discussion of "us" versus "them." It isn't about mindlessly following the moral directions of an elephant or a donkey. Being a follower of Jesus is about rejecting the polarization of our culture by realizing we are deeply moral beings who are meant to be put back together because we have been asked to help put the world back together. It's about realizing that "we" are here for "their" good.

TRUTH

When we are talking about morality, we are talking about the right way for humans to live, which means we are talking about truth. Like baby-dedication-guy and rock-star-activist-guy, the Biblical writers cared deeply for the idea of truth. The Hebrew word for truth is *emet*.

In Hebrew, *emet* is composed of three letters. It looks like this:

אמת

The first letter to far right is aleph.

The middle is mem.

And the far left is tav.

Aleph is the first letter of the Hebrew alphabet.

Mem is the middle letter.

Tav is the last letter.

First.

Middle.

Last.

Or we could say:

Right.

Middle.

Left.

Truth is a big topic. And the concept of *emet* kept the writers of the Bible conscious of the reality that humans need to give their whole being to seeing the whole picture. Personal piety is only part of the truth. So is social justice. Truth is simply too big to be splintered into left and right. It's too big to be claimed exclusively by those escalating our culture wars. Today, it's possible to sell tons of books by claiming we "stand for the truth." But unless our truth is big enough to care for our own souls and people who do not have clean water, Jesus wouldn't buy it.

Most of us grew up with the basic message that life was about being good. Either we became stuck there, convinced we are better than everyone else, or we grew tired of being good for shallow reasons that kept us isolated from the wider world. We ran out, smoked pot and said a few bad words just to prove we could do it and still be Christians. At the same time, we became intrigued with a lifestyle that was about making the world a little bit more bearable. So we ran off to go do good works.

I write this chapter because I am convinced there is another option. It's the way of Jesus.

It's about crossing the line our world has set up between personal and social morals.

It's about orphans and our souls.

It's about being good and then taking that goodness across the lake.

It's about being good—and being good for something.

This is a scary chapter to write. Often when elephants and donkeys are brought into a discussion, someone alleges a conspiracy of some sort. Sometimes it's the deeply religious that have cultivated this habit to its full potential. But that is to forget that the Jesus movement is itself a conspiracy. It's a divine conspiracy for putting the world and the individual back together. It's a conspiracy that starts with Christmas.

THE THEOLOGY OF FIRST CHRISTMAS LIVING

CHAPTER 5

CHAPTER 5 |

THEOLOGY OF FIRST CHRISTMAS LIVING

My wife Savannah is the greatest person I know. I would highly recommend marriage to anyone, as long as you marry a better person than yourself. In college, she spent a lot of her free time befriending foreign-exchange students like a young woman named Penny, who came from China. They both attended a private Christian university in the middle of Arkansas. There, many of the exchangers came from the Far East, so central Arkansas proved to be a bit of a culture shock (like it is for most of us). When Penny arrived at college, she was quickly immersed in a community of Christians. During her first year in the country, well-intentioned people did their best to convince Penny to become a follower of Jesus. They came up with every convincing claim and clever proof and compelling argument. It wasn't effective. It was an overwhelming experience, and she eventually came to the conclusion that Christians were pushy, strange people.

It's a sad story, but it's common. We love the picture of Jesus going to the other side of the lake or some other similar image, and we want to do the same kind of things. We want to make things better. We want other people to truly live. We want people to have what we are experiencing. We want our tribe to grow. So we set off for the far side of the lake, or maybe the other side comes to us. We have no idea what to do. We reach for the only things we know.

Proofs.

Claims.

Ideas.

Words.

Arguments.

T-shirts with giant crosses.

Guaranteed conversion curriculums.

Threats.

Methods like these usually come from well-intentioned hearts that don't know better. But we need to ask the question, "Is this how the life of God is meant to be shared?"

THE FIRST CHRISTMAS

For most of us, the image of the original Christmas celebration is filled with wise men, feeding troughs, and the birth of Jesus. While that is original, Jesus' birthday wasn't celebrated until hundreds of years after his birth. The first Christians celebrated many other sacred days and events, reminding them of the ways God had acted in the world and the ways he was still acting, but no Christmas. For some reason, it wasn't as important as other things. But then around the year of 350 AD, the first celebration of Christmas shows up on December 25. Why so late in the history of the Church and why on that date?

For the first part of the Church's existence, Christianity was a minor-league religion. Small groups of people worshipped Jesus in secluded corners of the Roman Empire. The big religions of the day were known as mystery cults or mystery religions. They were called "mystery" religions because they had secret initiation rituals. One of the largest of the mystery cults centered on the worship of Mithra, the sun god.[79]

Mithra or some variation of him was central to many ancient religions. People understood the relationship the sun had with all forms of life on the planet. Lots of sun meant lots of life (primarily in the form of food). No sun meant no life (no food). Since humans were aware of their dependence on the sun, it was only natural that some would worship it.

The worshippers of Mithra were highly in tune with seasonal changes. As the days grew shorter and the shadows longer, the members of the cult would bring in evergreen limbs and light candles. The candles and the greenery symbolized the sun and the planet it fed. Since everything was dying outside, they wanted a way of bringing life into their homes. This practice continued until the winter solstice (usually around December 24 or 25 on the Julian calendar), the shortest and darkest day of the year. Since the days grew longer from then on, worshippers celebrated that date as Mithra's birthday.[80]

Now of course much of the imagery from this event sounds strangely common. The date and the décor are both familiar. Often when people learn this, they jump to ask a lot of the wrong questions. Is it okay to celebrate Christmas? Is it pagan to put up lights and greenery? Is this why the words "Santa" and "Satan" are just one letter different?[81]

What we miss is an important picture into an ancient way of dealing with issues. To the first Christians, the worship of Mithra was not the best way to live. It wasn't the truest take on the universe. It was a distortion of reality. It was a way of thinking and living that could lead a person down a dark path. But what did they do about it? They decided to celebrate Jesus' birth on the very same day, in an identical way. Why?

There were multiple options. They could have protested, argued, or fought. They could have set up a totally different day at the opposite end of the calendar with decorations no one would have associated with another god. But instead the early Christian movement celebrated Jesus' birth on Mithra's day in Mithra's way. This is sacred ground. The early Christians did not see their mission as setting up a totally separate reality, isolated from the world. They decided to take something false and reorient it around something true. They took a broken idea and did their best to put it back together.

That sort of approach to life takes courage. It is easy to call out wrong attitudes in people who are far removed from our daily routine, people we know little about and who know little about us. It is easy to draw the line between us and them and then talk about them in demeaning ways.

Interestingly, historians have no clear date when the celebration of Mithra ended and the celebration of Jesus eclipsed it. It took over a century. There was no quick fix, no magic words, no guaranteed conversion curriculum. It was a slow, subtle subversion.

To take something false and reshape it around something true means believing in a God who said his kingdom was like a small seed that would eventually grow. It takes patience. It takes imagination. It means we have to live close to the problems in the world if we are going to subvert them. It means we have to respect people and their lifestyles if we are going to make Christmases out of Mithra birthdays.

But even if we celebrate Jesus' birth on the twenty-fifth of December because of the early Church and if the difference between the two celebrations had nothing to do with décor, the ritual, or the date (if it had nothing to do with anything external), well, then, what was so convincing? It was the people of course. This approach wasn't new.

NOT A WORD

In the Book of Romans, Paul writes, "Don't be overcome with evil, but overcome evil with good."[82] It's a brilliant line. For Paul and the first Christians, it wasn't just clever literature. It was a way of life. Paul spent much of his life confronting destructive tendencies and warped world-views, like the worship of Mithra.

For about two years, Paul called a city named Ephesus home.[83] Ephesus was a large port city that made a huge amount of money off of trade. With trade came people from diverse corners of the globe. With those people came their religions. Ephesus became known for its rich cultic life. At the center of this scene was the Temple of Artemis, the goddess of fertility.

The worship of Artemis was less than G-rated. Worshippers would offer some form of animal sacrifice, and then go around to the back side of the temple. There they found an open patio restaurant with other worshippers seated. A meal made from the sacrifice would be served followed by lots of wine, followed by an orgy—a great family outing. Just like the worship of Mithra, it was a dark distorted way to live. It made things worse and warped the way people understood themselves and the world.

And this is where Paul decides to put down roots.

For around two years, Paul works hard during the day, spends the evenings discussing the new life God had to offer, and gains friends along the way. At the close of the two years, something strange happens. No one is going to Artemis' temple anymore.

The Temple of Artemis was not only a center of religious activity; there was an economy to go along with it.[84] The temple had some sort of primitive gift shop, where small statues of Artemis could be purchased and taken home as souvenirs. At the end of Paul's second year, a silversmith named Demetrius who worked in the statue-maker union begins to complain that their business is hurting due to a lack of patronage. He blames the loss of business on Paul. In just two years, people stopped buying the idols, which means they stopped going to the temple, which means they stopped worshipping Artemis.

With an economy on the brink, Demetrius is able to gain some support for his position. Before long a mob forms and detains some of Paul's friends. Most people don't know why they are even participating in the riot. The situation grows to the point where the city is in danger of getting in trouble with the Roman Empire. The mayor of the city appears before the mob and states:

> Men of Ephesus, doesn't all the world know that the city of Ephesus is the guardian of the temple of the great Artemis? Therefore, since these facts are undeniable, you ought to be quiet and not do

anything rash. You have brought these men here, though they have neither robbed temples, nor blasphemed our goddess.[85]

It is a mayor doing his best to keep his job and keep his city out of trouble. But his speech betrays to us Paul's subversive lifestyle. After two years, the Christians never "blasphemed" Artemis. This means that although they didn't agree with the lifestyle or worldview in Ephesus, they never criticized it. Paul didn't spend his time slamming Artemis or the lifestyle that such worship advocated. He never provided a list of proofs for why Jesus was real and Artemis a sham. The followers of Jesus didn't sit around making jokes about Artemis and the people who worshipped her. They didn't threaten people with following Jesus or else facing the prospect of being well done in the afterlife. Yet, in just two short years, huge portions of the population had left Artemis for Jesus.

Paul understood what we struggle to grasp; people are not inspired to believe by reactionary words and critical remarks. People don't want to be threatened, scolded, or made fun of because they believe and live differently. Paul understood that people are tempted to believe in something bigger than Artemis when they are given a glimpse of something better. For two years, Paul and his buddies lived proactively. They worked, served, gave, ate, loved, and yes, even talked a bit in a way that enticed people to suspect the tomb was empty, and that was all the convincing Ephesus ever needed.

FISHING

Most of us grew up with other messages though. We were told to be "fishers of men."[86] This usually meant going door to door and offering people compelling arguments as to why people ought to be Christians. It's a phrase that comes straight from Jesus as he invites some young Jewish fishermen to be his disciples. But it's a difficult metaphor. When you fish for fish, you yank them out of the water, kill them, and eat them—the fish and the fishermen aren't exactly on the same team. Maybe this partially explains why it's easy to adopt a confrontational posture towards the world. Whatever the case, this reality wasn't lost on those fishermen.

In the Jewish Scriptures, God is referenced twice as a fisherman. In both texts, fishing has to do with punishment. In Jeremiah, God says, he will "catch" unfaithful Israelites that are working against his purposes and send them off to exile.[87] In Ezekiel, God says he will "hook" Egypt, the empire that enslaved Israel and continued to entice it.[88] Twice God is portrayed as an angler. Twice vengeance and violence are mentioned. No wonder those fishermen left their nets. In a world where Jews were being heavily taxed and driven off their land by foreigners, who wouldn't want in on that sort of fishing?

One of those fishermen was named Simon, son of Jonah. In the ancient world, names told a story; they reflected character. Look at the names a family gave their children over generations, and it's easy to plot their past politics as well as their future ambitions. "Simon" is a name that comes from an early Jewish revolutionary who, years before, overthrew the ruling pagan empire and granted Israel a few years of self-rule. "Jonah" was the reluctant prophet who anxiously longed for his enemies' destruction while fearing God's inclination for mercy. This family is a group of people who not only fish for a living, but who are waiting for God to do some fishing of his own. They were waiting for God to push and shove to make a better world. With the cultivation of such a confrontational posture, Simon could not ignore Jesus' offer.[89]

But Jesus has other ideas than changing the current world order through vengeance. Immediately after Jesus recruits the fishermen, he proceeds to heal both a leper and a paralytic, and lastly befriend and include a hated tax-collector named Matthew (there is a good chance Matthew previously embezzled funds from Simon). In a world where sickness is a sign of divine curse, Jesus offers divine healing. In an age where selling out your heritage for money, like Matthew had, is unforgiveable, Jesus offers belonging. Jesus' reinterpretation of "fishing" means "fishing for men" has little to do with fishing. It has less to do with conflict or violent confrontation. It's about making things better, even for those we think are the enemy.

IN OR OUT

The religious leaders in Jesus' world understood the boundary between "us" and 'them" to be rigid and fixed. If you were "in," it was clear. You believed certain things. You acted a certain way. You dressed a certain way.[90]

It was just as obvious if you were out. You didn't believe certain things. You behaved differently. You looked different. You were on the outside of this barrier if you were a different race, someone who was ill, or professionally immoral. You could come into the community if you changed and believed. Essentially, you could come and get it. The institution that certified your admission was the Temple in Jerusalem, the place where Jews believed heaven and earth met, the place from where God's love and justice would one day fill the earth.

But when Jesus was "fishing for people," he seemed to be including everyone on the outside. He befriended corrupt officials and immoral women. He healed foreigners' children and touched the unclean. But these weren't just good works. These were statements. Jesus was messing with the boundary, without the help of the Temple.

What seemed like an inflexible stationary boundary to everyone else, Jesus saw as mobile and elastic. This is why Jesus traveled around including all the wrong sorts of people in the community of God. Those who once saw themselves outside suddenly sensed they were "in." But these people couldn't change their beliefs and habits immediately. They weren't asked to get everything straight theologically and morally before they joined Jesus' community. They were invited to belong long before they believed or behaved. They were renamed from "out" to "in" because to Jesus, the line between "us" and "them" is as portable as God needs it to be.

Along the way something happened to the misfits who joined Jesus. They began to believe. Eventually they began to behave. Then they changed the world. What started as belonging led to being repaired, which led to repairing. In fact, one early writer described the Jesus movement as "God's building,"[91] that is, the Temple. The misfits and sinners transformed into being the place where heaven and earth collide, the place from where God's love and justice fill creation.

It's brilliant—and it's needed badly today. This doesn't mean that we give up our standards and become relativists or whatever else we're afraid of. It simply means we understand what Jesus did, that healing and change comes through visible demonstrations of love, not by jumping through hoops.

If you're a Christian, this is what happened to you. God invited us to belong long before we believed. If we're honest, we're all still learning how to live. We're still learning how to behave. If that is a gift we have been given, then we don't have to strut around like we've got it all nailed down. We can allow the gift accepted to become the gift extended. That's what the first Christmas and Paul's years in Ephesus were all about.

I'LL HAVE A PINT OF THAT

The most compelling evidence for Jesus is a welcoming embrace or the encounter with someone truly alive, not an invitation to come and get it. Think back to the moment when you were ready to say, "The tomb is empty and everything is beginning again." It probably was not at the close of being threatened about your post-mortem destination or pressured by a clever argument. For most of us, our journey to God began when we met a person who seemed to be plugged into something bigger. The way they lived and loved moved us to say, "Whatever he's drinking, I'll have a pint of that."[92]

People are always more convincing than words. As a very old, very dead Christian once said, "Christianity is not about convincing people of particular ideas, it is about inviting them to share in the greatness of Christ."[93] Following Jesus is a way of life, not simply a system of thinking or believing or voting. It's about the genuine human experience of being repaired and repairing. It's about being loved and then loving. It's a journey of people who are compelled to believe that there is someone in the world who is working to make everything right and, as they join in the work, inviting others to come along for the ride.

MOM

My mom is one of my spiritual heroes. She and my dad blazed a trail of faith for my family. She possesses a deep connection with God. But a little over a year ago my mom was diagnosed with cancer. I will always remember sitting next to her just after she received the news as she said, "I just don't know where God is anymore." It was understandable. Her life took a frightening turn and uncertainty loomed large. There were a lot of people around her who quoted Bible verses and told her how she should feel. She had doctors trying to diagnose her physical illness, and others trying to diagnose her emotional distress.

The next few months were long and wearisome, with visits to the doctor, treatments, and worry. During her last chemotherapy treatment before returning to normal life, she reflected on her doubts about God's presence. She said, "I didn't know where God had gone. But after all the kindness, after all the prayers, after all the love, I realized he was right next to me all along." For my mom, God didn't show up in the diagnosis or in the people telling her how to feel and think and what Bible verses to quote. God showed up in the loving embrace of people who were willing to be there and simply join in her struggle.

For many, God is a vague concept. He often proves too abstract to make the sort of progress we desire. We wish we could get a clear picture of him. A burning bush would be nice, or perhaps a miracle that doesn't involve paying a televangelist. But like John says, "No one has ever seen God, but when we love one another, God lives in us and his love comes to complete expression through us."[94] It's as if the writer is saying, God can be invisible and confusing but when we find the courage to love genuinely, the invisible God becomes visible. The unseen is seen.

WHAT ABOUT BOB?

If you haven't seen the movie *What About Bob?*, you are not truly human. Stop reading this book, rent the movie, watch it, and then come back. Now that you've shared the joy, you know it's a movie about a character named Bob Wiley. Bob is a paranoid schizophrenic who has no family, no friends, and no connections to a healthy life aside from his relationship with his goldfish, Gill.

After exhausting some of New York's finest psychiatrists, Bob meets up with Dr. Leo Marvin. During their first appointment, something about Leo convinces Bob that he can be cured. As the initial interview ends, Leo retreats to his office to record his diagnosis. He says Bob is a "multi-phobic personality suffering from acute separation anxiety with extreme need for family connections." Bob has issues that Leo diagnoses with great precision. Essentially Bob is dysfunctional because he doesn't have anyone. Beyond the medical vocabulary is the reality that Bob needs people.

As the movie progresses, Leo leaves for vacation with his family while Bob stalks along uninvited. As Bob performs the role of the uninvited guest, the doctor who brilliantly diagnosed Bob as needing friends is unable to be one. Yet the rest of Leo's family takes Bob under their wing. The crossing of professional boundaries pushes Leo over the edge. As the movie unfolds, Bob comes to life as Leo loses his mind. It's funny. But there is a message. The brilliance needed to make a diagnosis is worthless unless you're willing to be part of the cure.

Whenever I watch *What About Bob?*, I can't help but reflect on our current situation in American spirituality. We are tempted to think that being right is the most important thing. We make diagnoses about the plight of our world and the dysfunction of those around us. We have endless blogs, books, and radio shows dedicated to convincing ourselves of how correct we are. There is an air of condescension about it, as if simply diagnosing a social or personal ill is heroic. To be part of the repair of our world, we can't afford to be patronizing. We can't be Leo Marvin.

We need the humility and genuine concern to realize what our ancient brothers and sisters did. Whether it was Christmas or Ephesus or my mom's battle with cancer, we need to understand healing and repair comes from God through humans able to love and befriend and support those in trouble and those who are causing trouble. Sometimes the world that we love to diagnose just needs a hand to hold.

PENNY

Despite her initial impressions, Penny, my wife's friend from China, became a Christian. A few years after that, Savannah and I had the good fortune of spending the holidays with her. After a fun evening of looking at Christmas lights, the three of us found ourselves in a coffee shop enjoying a game of Connect 4. I wanted to know more about Penny's story, so I asked her, "What was it that convinced you?" She said, "After the first few months, people stopped trying to convert me. I think they gave up. But for the next few years, I lived with them, I watched them. They invited me to dinner, took me places, bought me groceries. Then one day I asked myself, *These people. What makes these people so different?* And that was it. I knew I wanted to be a Christian."

Christianity is not about defending the borders of our faith. It is about celebrating what is at the center of reality. It is about allowing that celebration to be so infectious and true that others can't help but think, "Whatever they're drinking, I'll have a pint of that." It's about living close enough to our time's Ephesus that we can paint a picture of something better. It's about knowing modern worshippers of Mithra so we can offer something better to celebrate.

It's the holidays again, and today my family is putting up our Christmas decorations. The days are growing shorter and the shadows longer. The chill in the air is contrasted by the warmth of our home. As we put up the tree and lights, I find myself proud to be part of a movement that thinks it best to take ugly things and make them beautiful. I feel privileged to be a part of a movement that subverts through love. I feel hopeful that we can still redraw the lines around a world that has been told it's "out" and needs to jump through hoops if it wants to belong. I believe Christians have something priceless to contribute. The world can be a cold and dark place, but thank God, we have many more Christmas memories left to make.

MARRIAGE AS METAPHOR

CHAPTER 6

MARRIAGE AS METAPHOR

For many years marriage was a frightening idea. It wasn't the commitment that was frightening. It was frightening because it looked like a trick. The trick went something like this:

People meet.

People become friends.

People have hormones.

Hormones meet.

People get overwhelmed emotionally.

People start thinking about the joy of starting a new life.

People decide to do the married thing.

(Partially because they are excited about doing the sex thing.)

People get married.

People slowly find out you can't have sex all day.

People slowly find out your feelings of infatuation are unsustainable.

People find out starting a new life is harder than they imagined.

People wonder why they got married.

Sure, this isn't a fair representation. This is just what I thought marriage was like. I had the ammunition to back it up. Although my parents have a great marriage, I witnessed plenty of my contemporaries walk down the aisle with emotions and hormones cheering them on. Eventually, I saw those emotions and hormones subside, and I saw a lot of good people grow dismayed with the results. Some of them got on with life reluctantly and made it work. Some stayed miserable. Some ended the venture. With that, I thought it was a big trick. My main objection was that I simply did not see any larger point.

Everything changed while having a conversation with an old friend. In an instant, I saw her in a new way. There are no words to explain that moment or the many that followed. I'm hoping you've had or will have that experience, too. It's something deeper and subtler and more wonderful than the cynical distortion of love I described a moment ago. I realized this is why so many of my friends took that huge step into the unknown. But even if all the marriages in the world were propelled by moments like mine, it didn't change the fact that a lot of them end desperate and dreary. I still wasn't sold. I needed direction. I needed a better picture of marriage.

Insight arrived when I understood marriage as a metaphor. In the Bible, Paul instructs husbands and wives to get along. He tells wives to respect their husbands, as they do God. Husbands are to sacrifice their lives for their wives as Jesus did for the world. It's Paul's way of saying when a couple serves each other passionately, marriage can be fulfilling. It's a great idea and many problems could be solved right here with the whole mutual submission lifestyle. But then Paul's trajectory veers as he writes:

> For this reason, "a man will leave his father and mother and be united to his wife, and the two will become one flesh." This is a profound mystery— but I am talking about Christ and the Church.[95]

So we think it's about Frank and Sue and how they need to function within their marriage. But is it really about Jesus and you and me? Yes. Marriage is a metaphor. Two people getting hitched is meant to function as a picture of a larger cosmic reality.

The whole "man leave his parents" thought is not original to Paul. He actually borrowed the phrase from an ancient text in Genesis. Back at the beginning of the story, God created the world and called it "good." The world isn't finished, it's not complete, it's not perfect. In order for creation to become all that God dreams, he creates a man. This man is to "work and to watch."[96] Meaning that God delegated responsibility to the first man to step into the creative process and further the creation of the world. But a problem appears. God says, "It is not good for man to be alone. I will make a helper suitable for him."[97] This is the first mention of something in creation that is not good.

Up to this point, each facet of the creation had a role to fulfill, and each role was energized with God's blessing. God gave some aspect of creation a task and then provided the energy to accomplish it. But God realized Adam was given a massive job that he simply couldn't complete alone.

So God initiates a parade as all of the animals file past Adam. Adam names them, but "for Adam no suitable helper was found."[98] Which means a dog can be a great companion, but not much help. Out of this predicament, God makes woman out of Adam. When the two meet for the first time, Adam launches into song, most likely R&B:

> This is bone of my bones
> and flesh of my flesh;
> she shall be called "woman"
> because she was taken out of man.[99]

These words mean that Adam is now convinced the "not good" situation is resolved. He has a partner. This doesn't mean she is subordinate in any way. This is a partnership. Who's in charge is not part of the equation. They are equal. Together, the job of caring for and watching over the world can happen.

Marriage then is about two beings that function as one being because they are meant to complete a sacred task. This task of caring for the world is too big for either one of them alone. Marriage is about partnership. Marriage is about making the impossible possible.

The picture we are given is one of collaborative dependency. This isn't the insecure dependency that ruins many relationships. It is as if there is a reciprocal cry at the center of a marriage that says, "I cannot be who I am supposed to be and I cannot do what I am meant to do without you. Our worst day together is better than our best day alone."

Which is different than the cry that often fuels relationships which says, "I cannot function unless you tell me every second how important I am to you and spend all your time with me. I am needy. That's why I wanted to date you. I can't ever get enough attention from you to make myself feel valuable. So you have a lifetime of unproductive hell ahead of you as you try to meet my needs. Good luck."

Romance and intimacy are a huge part of this original design. It isn't just about partnering in a great cause, as if it's a business deal. To commit to collaborating for the betterment of the world, souls will mingle. That means whole beings will come together. That means sex and romance.[100] Sometimes it will be for comfort. Sometimes it will be for celebration. Sometimes it will be for appreciation. The posture of a marriage is at times face to face. But it's always in the context of something bigger. If intimacy doesn't translate into standing shoulder to shoulder in service before the world, then the marriage is missing something.

Marriage is about his love for her, and her love for him, growing into their gift to others. Ask parents who have a child. Their love is now about something bigger than the two of them. That is the point. Marriage is supposed to make a baby. Whether that baby is a well in Africa, a group of people you care for, or simply "little Weston," marriage is always about something bigger.

Which brings us back to the passage we started with. Like this chapter, it has more to do with us and God, than Frank and Sue.

After all, marriage is a metaphor. It is a way of pointing to a larger cosmic reality. Marriage gives insight into how Jesus and his followers are to relate. This perhaps is why a clear vision of marriage is so central, because it revolutionizes our understanding of our place in the universe.

If marriage is about collaborative dependency, and if marriage is about two beings becoming one entity to make a contribution to the world, then what does that mean about us and God?

It means God is looking for a partner.[101]

If this is how things are meant to be, then we need to ask, "How exactly do we collaborate with God?"

Great question.

Here are some hints.

SUFFERING

In one place, Paul writes to his friends, "For just as the sufferings of Christ flow over into our lives, so also through Christ our comfort overflows."[102]

Suffering is a tough subject. When you live in a world where leisure functions as a magic potion, suffering becomes the enemy. It is easy to get caught up in all that nonsense. Messages exist that portray Jesus' sufferings as though he was a cosmic piñata, whose beatings provide the rest of the world a painless, private spirituality.

But that is not the language of Christianity. Paul senses that in some way he is experiencing the same sufferings as Jesus. For some strange reason, Paul indicates that this is a good thing. Because as Paul suffers like Jesus, he also receives some sort of strange comfort as well. This comfort isn't just for him. It overflows. It makes life better for his friends. It seems like a foreign idea, but there it is at the heart of Christianity. Suffering leads to comfort. Pain leads to healing.

Where would Paul ever pick up such an idea?

Paul was originally known as Saul to the Jewish community.[103] He was a popular upstart within an ancient religious sect known as the Pharisees. They were a group of influential men who were known for their passion for the Torah and their frustration with the current world order. Israel was occupied by the ruthless empire of Rome. Jews were taxed heavily, and Israel itself kept sliding deeper and deeper into debt. This debt meant that many Jews were losing their ancestral family lands to large, sometimes Jewish, sometimes non-Jewish, conglomerates. This forced certain Jews to take drastic (often violent) measures to voice their displeasure, which in turn gave the Roman military machine an excuse to execute greater brutality. It was a vicious cycle. For a Pharisee, there was only one explanation. Israel was not living up to her end of the deal.

If Israel was God's nation and the occupying forces and other ethnicities of the world were not, then something was terribly wrong. The Pharisees concluded that their current suffering was caused by Israel's failure to follow the Torah properly. The Torah functioned as the marriage contract between God and Israel, and since the situation on the ground was deteriorating, the obvious conclusion was that Israel had broken her vow. Paul's hope along with his colleagues was that once Israel lived out the marriage contract properly, God would send a Messiah, military revolution would follow, and Israel could beat up on her enemies.

For Saul, suffering was a sign of failure.

A better world could only be made when their pain was felt by others.

A healthy partnership between God and Israel would involve the suffering of other people.

This is why so many in Jesus' world could never accept him as the hoped for Messiah. After all, he was executed by the evil empire. He suffered a violent death. Suffering was a sign of failure. The whole claim that he rose from the dead didn't make sense, and it didn't matter because God's people were still suffering. The world was still a mess.

So years after Jesus' ministry, Saul terrorizes the region, inflicting suffering on those who claim allegiance to a suffering Messiah. As Saul makes a trip north to a city called Damascus, Jesus appears to him. They have a little conversation. Saul walks away ready to admit he needs to rethink his vision of a violent partnership with God.

As Saul travels towards the city, God sends word to a fellow named Ananias that Saul is on the way. Ananias is alarmed because he perceives Saul as a terrorist. This isn't much of a stretch, since Saul is a terrorist. But God tells Ananias:

> "This man is my chosen instrument to carry my name before the Gentiles and their kings and before the people of Israel. I will show him how much he must suffer for my name." [104]

Jesus is going to show Saul how much he must suffer?

He is going to suffer for God, not inflict suffering for God?

Somehow this is going to make things better?

But this is how it was supposed to be.

Hundreds of years earlier the prophet Isaiah wrote,

Surely he took up our infirmities and carried our sorrows, yet we considered him stricken by God, smitten by him and afflicted. But he was pierced for our transgression, he was crushed for our iniquities; the punishment that brought us peace was upon him.[105]

Isaiah caught another vision of suffering. It was the suffering of someone who would come and take responsibility for everyone else's mess. Though the cost for taking ownership over the world's junk would be immense, it would have a mysterious effect. It would bring people peace. In the Hebrew language the word for peace is *shalom*. In our minds peace usually means an absence of conflict. But to the Jewish mind, *shalom* means wholeness or healing or repair.[106] *Shalom* is about restoring the whole created order to its original design.

Suffering would be redemptive.

This was the vision at the heart of Jesus' ministry. The Gospels record a Jesus who spent his life articulating and demonstrating the life the world was always meant to enjoy. In his healing of those with physical ailments or teaching brilliant messages about the fullness of life, Jesus was connecting humans to a truer reality. In his own community of followers, he invited victims and their oppressors, like poor fisherman and tax collectors, to find new ways to live together.[107] Jesus was about bringing in the *shalom* of God.[108] But the path of Jesus was different from other more popular paths. That brought Jesus into sharp contrast with the people and institutions that offered rival ways of living and thinking. Conflict was inevitable.

When you go around saying the Kingdom of God is for the poor[109] while the economy is propped up by exploitation, it sounds dangerous. When one part of the religious establishment is busy making a buck off the vulnerable masses while the other is beating the war drum and you flip over their registers[110] and say things like "love your enemy,"[111] it sounds like a challenge. When the leaders of your society obsess over splitting the whole world into classes of "in" and "out" and you start a movement with members of both groups, it sounds like a threat to the whole system. When you call out the bull that runs most of our world, you're going to get the horns. That is what happened to Jesus in three short years.

As Jesus makes his way south towards Jerusalem for one final Passover celebration, it is obvious he is on a collision course with the forces that use violence and suffering as a means to shape the world. The anticipation in his contemporaries' minds reaches a fever pitch. It's Passover, after all. Passover celebrates the memory of God's rescue of Israel from slavery. But the celebration isn't simply about looking back. It is also about looking forward. What God did for his people in Egypt, he will do again. Everyone is wondering if that future hope is about to become a present reality.

This is why crowds welcomed him a week before Passover with palm branches. A few generations before Jesus, the Jewish nation used the palm branch as the symbol of a bloody quest for independence from the occupying forces.

As Jesus and his friends sit down to share the customary Passover meal, revolution hangs in the air. No doubt hundreds if not thousands of his countrymen await the word to draw their swords. But as the meal gets underway, Jesus takes the bread and says, "Take and eat, this is my body."[112] After the meal, he takes a cup of wine and says, "This is my blood of the covenant, which is poured out for many."[113] Jesus is stating, "Tonight is the night. The revolution is in fact about to happen. The New Exodus is here." But in a brilliant reinterpretation, this revolution is not going to happen the way everyone anticipated. Jesus says the revolution would happen as he is "broken" and "poured," which is different from the hope of "breaking" and "pouring" everyone else.

Jesus wasn't planning to launch a revolt like many had envisioned. Instead, he planned to allow the forces that dehumanize and disgrace the world to do their very worst to him. That was the plan. That was the revolution. The *shalom* of God was going to come about through experiencing suffering, not by inflicting it on others. Instead, Jesus set up his rule, as one writer says it, by "the blood of his cross."[114] Which sounds like a failure.

But Jesus understood something profound. Larger catapults and smarter bombs do not make the world a better place, because they cannot deal with the real problem. Like all our novel forms of power and force, they only make the world better for one person at the expense of another. The use of fighter jets, sweatshops, and terrorism simply agrees with the premise that creation is nothing more than a wrestling mat for people who want power and control. The cycle cannot be stopped by more munitions. Someone will always come up with a larger weapon or more exploitative economic policy. Someone has to take responsibility for the mess we have made. Someone has to own it. Someone has to suffer. This world is a God-breathed sacred place, not a wrestling mat.

That was Isaiah's vision all along.

That's what Jesus decided to do.

Because that is the only hope the world has.

So Jesus is arrested and executed. He suffers a horrific death at the hands of people who imagine a better world lay on the other side of violence and suffering.

They were right, but not in the way they imagined. To the shock of everyone, Jesus came back to life a few days later. He rose as a new species of human. Healed. Repaired. Whole. Indestructible.

IT'S ONLY THE BEGINNING

The general belief in Jesus' world was that one day everything would be healed and repaired. The assumption was that such a day lay at the end of time and would occur through the means of violence as deity and the pious partnered to bomb evil into submission. But here it is, a repaired human, who came to reality not because he "broke and poured" others, but because he was "broken and poured" on behalf of our mess.

When the early Christians came in contact with the risen Jesus, they worshipped him as the ruler of the world, but they also walked away convinced that Jesus' repair was only the beginning of the repair of creation. As one author sang it, Jesus is "the firstborn over all creation."[115] Just as the harvest yields an early crop in advance of a larger one, Jesus' victory was the beginning of a whole new world. If Jesus is the "firstborn," it means the larger plan is unfinished. That means we have a role to play. After all, it's about a marriage.

Not long after his resurrection, Jesus told his followers, "As the Father sent me, so I am sending you."[116] Although Jesus' accomplishment is unique and world-changing, his method of dealing with the dysfunction in the world is an essential part of his movement. This is the way God's people were always meant to fulfill their end of the marriage contract. Suffering is not a sign of failure. Suffering is a part of the journey towards repair. When humans suffer on behalf of the mess in our world, it unleashes the energy of repair.

Darkness gives way to light.

Suffering births healing.

Death yields to life.

This is what Paul is alluding to when he speaks of Jesus as a husband. Those who met the risen Jesus sensed that he was sort of like a groom looking for a bride. This is why Jesus said Paul had to suffer and why Paul perceived his suffering was used by God to launch a strange healing for others. Jesus started the journey towards repair, but there is still a lot of pain in the world. Jesus is looking for someone who will own the pain of the world just like him. Jesus is looking for a partner.

This means being a Christian can never be about:

> voting the problems of the world away,

> or protesting immoral people out of our city,

> or hiding out in your bunker listening to people tell you how bad things are,

> or criticizing everything that you don't like,

> or imagining the world is about "us" versus "them."

Not too long ago, I met a high school science teacher who wanted to share his story. He was a determined Christian who went from school to school looking for the right fit. His first stop was at a school that didn't agree with his perspective on the origins of life. He believed the theory of evolution was evil and that the only reasonable alternative was God's creation of the world in seven literal days. So he went to another school and then another, where he finally found the right fit. It was a public school where all the teachers and administrators were Christians. He loved it because he could teach his understanding of how the world came to be and no one would object. He said it was great because he could "really ram it down their [the students'] throats."

This is something to celebrate?

Ramming a perspective down someone's throat?

As I listened to his story, I couldn't help but think that this is the exact way of thinking and living Jesus came to dismantle. It was obvious that this man had spent a considerable amount of mental and emotional energy to accomplish his vocational goals. This was his life's work. But, collaborating with God is never about "ramming" or "shoving" anything into anyone. Ramming and shoving is what has given the world its current shape. Doing it on behalf of Jesus is about as sad as it gets.

The belief in using force on God's behalf is not an anomaly limited to a few eras in history; it's more of a constant temptation. The Hebrew Bible is riddled with accounts of how God's community found itself tricked into trusting the ramming techniques of the latest empire.[117] It's during another empire-impersonating era that the prophet Isaiah envisions another type of spiritual community, one that teaches the nations how to "beat their swords into plowshares."[118] To give up on the dreams of empire and instead cultivate creation to its full potential is the daunting challenge given to every generation. But it's hard to get over our ramming habits.

I have a good friend named Patrick, who happens to live in sub-Saharan Africa. He is a prolific farmer and wonderful single parent, providing enough income for his three children to attend school. He works endlessly, drawing from a resourcefulness and determination that would put many to shame. When he invited me and some friends to his farm, I stood in awe of his accomplishments. I also noticed that over half of his land wasn't developed. The land could not be used because there was not enough water to irrigate the other half of his field. Patrick had dug by hand over fifty feet into the earth to get what water he had, but during the dry season, the well ran out.

If he possessed the finances to drill through bedrock, Patrick would have enough water to cultivate his entire field. This would lead to the hiring of people to help work his growing farm. The ground would be cultivated, so would the community. But Patrick can't afford such a luxury. His situation has nothing to do with lacking initiative. He lacks opportunity.

How many Patricks are there in the world? And how many over-zealous science teachers, who use their passions like swords? The Patricks of the world do not need people to use their energies like that; they need those swords to be converted to shovels—literally.[119]

There are a lot of good people wasting a lot of life attempting to partner with God through the sword. But that is how we get our way, not the way the world changes. Partnering with Jesus is about being tuned into how things are because we know how things will be. It is about allowing the pain of the world to become our pain. Not because it is altruistic or romantic or popular, but because this is how things change. We imitate a God who makes Easter Sundays out of Good Fridays, who makes a new world by taking responsibility for the mess of the old one, who makes order out of chaos, and life out of death. That is the marriage we are meant for, and it will make one beautiful kid.

MAKING BABIES

As Paul writes, "We know that the whole creation groans as in the pains of childbirth right up to the present time."[120] Half of the statement makes perfect sense. We know the world is groaning with every murder, famine, and ethnic cleansing. But these are the groans of a woman in labor? It sounds strange and slightly offensive to equate a vicious crime with the temporary pain of labor. But for Paul, when you stand on this side of an empty tomb, you can't help but become convinced that what happened to Jesus will happen to everything. It's unhealthy to deny the crippling pain in our world. But like a woman in labor, this pain is not the last word on our world. Like a woman in labor, the world's pain is going to end in great joy.

Paul continues, "Not only so, but we ourselves, who have the first fruits of the Spirit, groan inwardly as we wait eagerly for our adoption as sons, the redemption of our bodies."[121] So who is groaning? Are we groaning? Or is the world groaning? The answer is yes. Partnering with God is about being so close to the groans of the world that its groans become indistinguishable from our own. Since we know that the suffering world is salvageable, we are free to live in tune with her aches and pains.

But we also groan because we know we are not completely repaired ourselves. As it says, "we are waiting for our adoption." We are longing for our own final repair. This marriage is not about being a perfect moral agent. Collaborating with Jesus is about admitting we are groaning as we wait for God to put us completely back together. Since we are still being repaired, we are more than happy to join the world on her journey.

A repaired, healed, whole world is our baby. That is what our marriage to God is going to produce. Though the initiative is his, it is our job to meet the world in solidarity, joining in her suffering, and celebrating signs of new life. A Christian is somebody who is learning to "suffer and pray at the place where the world is its worst, so that it may be healed,"[122] just like Jesus.[123]

Such a task is meant for the creative and daring souls guided by the Spirit of Jesus.[124] It is our vocation to see problems and take ownership of them in healing ways. Whether it is tutoring a kid who is having trouble in school, adopting a child, working to restore a neglected neighborhood, or participating in microfinance, it answers the cry for collaborative dependency with an "I do." What matters is that we reject the temptation to tune out, pass the blame, or use "ramming" techniques. What matters is that we as individuals and communities carry the burdens of the world in such a way that we are willing to have our own blood, sweat, and tears drop to the ground on their behalf. That's the method used by Jesus. That's the way of repair.

THE CRIES OF OUR BABIES

I have some friends who live a life of suffering. They are a married couple who decided that they were meant to give their life to the special-needs community. They opened a camp in the middle of nowhere for kids with physical and developmental challenges. The camp gives kids from all over the world a week that every child deserves. There, kids with special needs become simply kids as they run, play, camp, paint, sing, and laugh and laugh and laugh. It is a little slice of heaven on earth. But, it is centered on suffering. Although my friends who started the camp and those who have joined the vision would never use such a word, it's true.

The couple who started that place gave up any hope of a normal life when they gave themselves to those kids. They have been faced with more difficulties and hurdles than any five couples put together. Then there are the campers. I am not sure if you have any contact with people with special needs. They are some of the greatest people I know, but the challenges they face are immense. To live in a world where the only people besides your parents who care about you are paid to do so is incredibly dehumanizing. It is hard to speak of the anguish and sacrifice of the parents of these kids. They empty their savings to pay medical costs, while spending every waking moment to care for their child's needs. Suffering. Suffering. Suffering.

But every summer in the middle of the Ozark Mountains, the parents get a week off, as the kids get to be kids. It's a great place. At the close of each day, something transcendent happens. Each night the whole place gets together to throw a wild party. It's a spectacle. Sometimes I walk a ways off and turn to see the sight from a different vantage point. From there you see people who are suffering. You see people who are suffering on behalf of the people who are suffering. Yet, no one seems like they are suffering. Late in the evening, in the midst of the twirling, singing, dancing, and laughing, something mysterious and magical happens. Somehow everyone's fears and hurts and insecurities get swallowed up in a celebration of life. Sometimes I close my eyes and listen to the sounds of the laughter and play, and just above it all I swear you can hear the cries of that new world being born.

My friends have a great marriage. They love each other, and yet their love has produced something that neither of them could do alone.

It's a great place.

Made by a great marriage.

But marriage is a metaphor.

WALKING DOWN WAVERLY TOWARDS EMMAUS

EPILOGUE

EPILOGUE |

WALKING DOWN WAVERLY TOWARDS EMMAUS

Speaking of marriages, there is a story in the Bible about a marital spat.[125] As a couple lumbers home, they find themselves at odds as they try to express complex emotions. Home is a small town called Emmaus. It isn't so much that they're ready to be home as much as they are ready to forget what happened behind them. A few days earlier in Jerusalem, their friend and rabbi Jesus was executed. It was a messy ending to their big dreams. In the complexity and sorrow, they express their feelings as only a married couple can.

Somewhere on their journey Jesus appears to the pair, only he's in disguise. Jesus asks, "What are you discussing?" They explain how they pinned their hopes on Jesus to be the Messiah and how he obviously wasn't if he got knocked off by the Romans. The journey to Jerusalem was filled with the hope that Jesus would launch the revolution for which they longed. Like we said, they even broke out the old palm branch routine, the symbol of military victory. Surely Jesus got the hint. Surely the moment had arrived when they, on God's behalf, could impose their political and moral agendas on the rest of the world. They were ready for the launch of a new world through fire and force. Now all those hopes are gone. To pour salt on the wound, bizarre stories are circulating about him coming back to life.

Jesus responds, "How foolish you are, and how slow of heart to believe all that the prophets have spoken! Did not the Christ have to suffer these things and then enter his glory?"

Then the writer goes onto say, "And beginning with Moses and all the Prophets, he explained to them what was said in all the Scriptures concerning himself."

The man and woman in the story were devout followers of Jesus. They travelled with him. They listened to his words. They witnessed his miracles. As good Jews, they spent their life reading the right sacred texts, going to the right religious services and practicing an uncompromising morality. But after all that, they still needed Jesus to "open the Scriptures" to them.

Their life was guided by a story, but it was a story that lost the plot. So Jesus "opened the Scriptures." Their whole life they understood being religious as creating a reality where the ugliness of the world was kept at arm's length. But this wasn't Jesus' understanding. Instead, Jesus insisted the plan for the "religious" all along was to be the place where the pain and suffering of the world intersected with the God who longed to roll up his sleeves and get involved, a God who wished to take responsibility, a God who would die and then rise. In his brilliance, Jesus simply retells the story.

It's a fascinating account that carries serious implications.

There is a large church in the city where I live that is finishing a multi-million dollar renovation of its facilities. The updates include a new coffee and juice bar.

At the same time, a statistic was released that revealed the very community that surrounds this church has a life expectancy fourteen years shorter than the American average. The reason is simple. No money. No doctors. No businesses. No transportation. No healthcare.[126]

As a kid, I remember sitting in church, knees knocking because of the prospects of eternity, lamenting the impending apocalypse, and unsure of what I was supposed to feel after praying that special prayer. Since then, I have come to realize that the same Stranger that visited our married couple has been journeying with me, retelling the story in fresh ways.

I am realizing that when the story is retold we find ourselves aching less for freshly squeezed juice after the service and aching more for the conditions in our world. Instead of a longing to go "there" after death, we find a passion for "there" to come "here." Instead of a life lived detached from the reality of our world, we discover energy to address things as they are. Instead of making waves in our world through various ramming methods, we find ourselves moved to take the pain of the world upon our shoulders. Instead of seeing the world as expendable and lost, we see it as repairable. That's the power of retelling the story. That's the power of rethinking.

I don't lead a large church. I'm not well known. I don't know how to surf. But just as that Stranger made sense of things on the road to Emmaus, I hope you've heard him speak again as we've made our way down Waverly. Like the repaired house that sits there after someone had the courage to see it from another perspective, Jesus invites us to see our world through the eyes of potential.

We need to do some rethinking.

Because Jesus invites us into a retelling of the story.

Because you and I have a role to play in re-creation.

ENDNOTES

1 The old Englishman was G.K. Chesterton. The metaphor appeared in his book *Orthodoxy*.

2 I think it's important to note that this was not my parents' doing or fault. It was all there was back in the day.

3 True story.

4 This is a clever allusion to the old series *Gilligan's Island*. I don't remember a single episode, but I remember the song about a "three-hour tour." I'm sure some people have never heard that song. It's also a hint that this is a short book, and it won't take you very long to read. But like the TV show about a boat ride that changed the passengers' lives, I'm hoping that this little read has some residual effects.

5 This phrase comes from Neil Postman and Charles Weingartner in *Teaching as a Subversive Activity*. The aphorism actually originates from Marshall McLuhan.

6 If you're my third grade teacher or that anesthesiologist, thanks for the metaphor and I forgive you.

7 Numbers 20.1–13

8 This works both ways. It isn't that we just follow our context mindlessly. We often play the devil's advocate by choosing the opposite of our parents' preferences or what is popular.

9 You should read Cartwright's *Diseases and Peculiarities of the Negro Race*.

10. It turns out that our "genital killer" didn't even attend the school he was defending.

11 As told by N.T. Wright in *Following Jesus: Reflections on Christian Discipleship*.

[12] This is really a fascinating subject. In the last two hundred years, many scholars have written about our strange predisposition to see reality subjectively and then search for objective facts to back up our perspective and our corresponding behavior. It seems to me like the concept was started by Ludwig Feuerbach.

[13] Usually projection is thought of in terms of externalizing negative feelings that a person cannot address consciously. Such as, when a person is determined to start World War II and then accuses Winston Churchill of the very thing he intends to do. A more everyday example would be a husband who cheats, but constantly accuses his wife of unfaithfulness.

[14] Exodus 3.13–14

[15] Many scholars have contributed to this interpretation but most of the above paragraph comes from Everett Fox's work, *The Five Books of Moses*.

[16] These are the indictments leveled by Isaiah, in 10.1–2. From his perspective, his society had created policies that were detrimental to the most marginal of society. According to Walter Bruggemann, the ruling class not only set up unjust laws, they set up a religious industry that sanctioned their actions and pacified the general population (Isa. 9.16).

[17] Isaiah 44.13

[18] This phrase comes from Peter Rollin's, *How Not to Speak of God*.

[19] Much of the work on the connection between idolatry and ideology comes from *How Not to Speak of God*.

[20] Inspired by a local church that spent a recent Sunday morning praying against the latest healthcare proposal. I was told about it by a friend, who is cancer patient, worried about paying for his healthcare.

[21] Exodus 7.1

[22] II Corinthians 5.20

[23] We see this ability to reflect the intelligence and wisdom of God in naming the animals. Name-giving is an act of God, and Adam is in some way grasping God's abstract ideas and transferring them to the flesh and blood Hippopotamus. As far as I know, this is my definition for stewardship (although I am known to think something was original with me only to find I stole it from someone unknowingly—that is why I openly claim this book to be filled with plagiarisms of all sorts). If this definition is somewhat original then and you happen to like it, feel free to steal it for your own book.

[24] Two items: One, I stole the phrase "faith of God" from John Ortberg, whom I respect immensely, but I just can't remember from where. Two, people may find this phrase troublesome in that it is extra-biblical. At the heart of the Bible and this book is the idea that God wants to reshape our understanding of the world around his own.

[25] I Corinthians 2.16

[26] I Thessalonians 5.21. Read the passage sometime. It is really remarkable. The instruction comes after Paul says, "Don't quench the Spirit" and "Don't treat prophecies with contempt." "Putting out the Spirit" and "treating ideas with contempt" happens when we become passive beings who swallow assumptions and don't put ideas to the test. In Paul's instance, he was referring to mindlessly following the propaganda of Rome.

[27] I would usually be uncomfortable to use two separate texts to make a single point. But both of these passages are from Paul and in both contexts the passages are about seeing the world correctly. Apparently it's possible. Apparently questioning is needed.

[28] Interview conducted on June, 5, 2007 by Giles Cayette, producer of "Space Shuttle Disaster," www.pbs.org/wgbh/nova/columbia/investigator.html.

Here are some interesting comments from Hubbard regarding the role assumption played in the disaster.

"They should have realized that something was wrong, but they didn't. Every computer coder in the world has a famous rule of thumb: 'Garbage in, garbage out.' Okay? And they put assumptions and numbers in there that had no connection with the kind of computer code it was.

"Over time, big organizations can fall into bad habits. And unless people insist on being absolutely rigorous, bad engineering can begin to take over. Day after day, you have to question assumptions; you have to ask yourself whether you have covered all the bases."

In the spring of 2003, the Columbia space shuttle launched on what was to be a routine mission. It wasn't until the next day while technicians reviewed tape of the launch that they realized something strange had happened. Eighty-one seconds into lift-off, a piece of foam used to insulate the main fuel tank had broken off and appeared to strike some portion of the left wing.

This had happened before. It was common knowledge that foam would sometimes break loose and hit the shuttle during launch. In the early days of the shuttle program, it was a concern. But after so many successful missions, the issue began to be ignored. Even though this piece of foam was much larger than other incidents in the past, those in charge of the mission determined that the wing was within the "margin of acceptable damage." It sort of made sense. It was foam after all.

There was "no concern for re-entry." The concern, if there had been room for any, would have been that the foam damaged the wing in some way. As the shuttle re-enters the atmosphere, it travels at over twenty-five times the speed of sound. As it hits the atmosphere, the molecules around the wing condense and heat to over 1600 degrees Celsius. The wing has to have the integrity to withstand the intensity of re-entry. If there is a problem with the integrity of the wing, the heat will prove too much and destroy the space shuttle.

The mission went on as scheduled. The astronauts were only told about the foam-strike in passing. It was mentioned for the purposes of public relations. The press knew about the foam. No one wanted an astronaut to seem like they didn't know the right answer when they returned. They never got the chance.

Somewhere over Texas, the space shuttle disintegrated, killing all seven astronauts.

Immediately after the crash, an investigation board was assembled to look into the cause of disaster. All the evidence pointed to a failure in the left wing, most likely the result of the foam. But how could foam do such damage? Scott Hubbard, the head of the investigation, staged a recreation of the situation by firing a similar piece of foam at a shuttle wing. The result was shock and sadness. The foam that wasn't a concern left a hole in the wing the size of a briefcase.

It was simple arithmetic really. A foam piece that weighs two pounds, moving at 500 miles per hour, would hit with over a ton of force. But how can an organization filled with scientists and engineers miss something that we learned (and then forgot) in high school?

The reasons were complex, but the investigation board ruled that NASA developed a "broken safety culture." This essentially means the organization had begun to run off of assumption instead of inquiry. Sometimes when a room full of people with credentials and clout get together, everyone starts assuming that they have the answers before the question is asked.

[29] For an interesting read about assumptions and presuppositions within the world of Jesus research, check out Ben F. Meyer's introduction to his work, *The Aims of Jesus.* Meyer states that the issue isn't simply about asking questions, but that humans

often work with a very limited number of possible answers. From those limited possibilities, humans form all sorts of dangerous presuppositions.

30 This is too clever of a phrase to come from me. But I have no idea where it came from.

31 Recently, I attended a political rally for a particular party. The whole ordeal lasted over three hours. In that time, not one person asked a single honest question. All the answers were settled beforehand, and we even found out that God explicitly endorsed their statements. Our job in the audience was to vote.

32 This quote along with many other ideas in this chapter is credited to Neil Postman and Charles Weingartner, *Teaching as a Subversive Activity.*

33 The "hope and history" line originates from Walter Bruggemann's *Hope within History.*

34 "Reign of Love." On Coldplay's *Viva La Vida or Death and All His Friends.*

35 I'm sure you are wondering about the naked-lady reference. It's there in Revelation 12. There it actually says she's dressed in the sun. I guess you have to credit a pre-adolescent imagination.

36 It's hard to tell if Darwin was the chicken or the egg. More than likely he was the egg. Before his adventures in the Galapagos, people like Malthus, Keats, and Hegel had already advanced the idea of social and political evolution. Darwin's research proved to be a real shot in the arm to the idea of progress.

37 This perspective is still very much alive today. There is a sentiment that religion and science are on an inevitable collision course. I highly recommend Stephen M. Barr's *Modern Physics and Ancient Faith.* Barr asserts that the intellectual debate is not between science and religion but between materialism and faith. Materialism is the philosophical position that the physical world is all there is and that matter behaves according to strict

mathematical rules. It's an opinion with large holes after the advent of quantum mechanics. When it comes to origins, the scientific debate is about method (using principles of observation to hypothesize, "How did turtles come into being?") not maker (meaning, "Is there something unobservable that could be behind the invention of turtles?").

[38] I am really not interested in answering the question of evolution vs. creation, because that issue is simply not at the heart of this story. I'm sure many people will have questions about using Genesis 1 against the backdrop of other Near-Eastern creation stories. But what sounds stranger: explaining this story in the context of the world it grew out of, or using it as proof for an argument that came thousands of years later? I was not present at the creation of the world. While I believe God is the creator of all, I cannot say what method he used to create.

[39] Before the time of Galileo, Thomas Aquinas stated, "With respect to the origin of the world, there is one point that is of the substance of faith, to know that it began at creation, on which all the authors in question are in agreement. But the manner and the order according to which creation took place concerns the faith only incidentally." We often think that only "liberal" "post-modern" authors accept a non-literal view of Genesis 1, but here we have a medieval orthodox saint acknowledging that this reality has existed through the ages. The reason for the ease in Aquinas' words is that Judaism and Christianity are not meant to be natural religions that try to explain all the facets of the natural world. They are not defined as faiths that refuse to accept the divinity of a tree or that a forest is haunted by spirits. Instead, they are faiths focused on the interface between God, humans, and the wider creation. What we think is the "old literalist reading" has gained prominence only in the fall-out from the Scopes Monkey Trial. Sure, the literal interpretation of Gen. 1 has been around a long time. But to those who hold such a position, Augustine writes

in *On the Literal Meaning of Genesis,* "Now it is a disgraceful and dangerous thing for a non-believer to hear a Christian, presumably giving the meaning of the Holy Scripture, talking nonsense on these topics, and we should take all means to prevent such an embarrassing situation, in which people show up vast ignorance in a Christian and laugh it to scorn. ... Reckless and incompetent expounders of Holy Scripture bring untold trouble and sorrow. ... To defend their utterly foolish and obvious untrue statements, they will try to call upon Holy Scripture ... although they understand neither what they say nor the things about which they make assertion. "

Both Aquinas and Augustine were pushing their own agendas, which usually had some Platonic edge, but it's still interesting that, for a long time, people have been open to discussing Genesis 1 from a variety of angles.

Much of the above is taken from Barr's book.

[40] We still need this as a society. This is why people of every country have some sort of story that proves beyond all doubt that God created them as unique and usually superior to others. I don't mean to suggest God is not behind creating nations, but that our versions of those stories usually end up like those of our ancient cousins, with power, control, and force being exercised over other lesser nations.

[41] What many of the stories such as "Enuma Elish" do is set Babylon up (or another nation) as the supreme race or tribe by describing the creation of the world and conquest of that creation by Marduk, who conveniently is also the chief deity of Babylon.

[42] The major stories that are studied as parallels to Genesis 1 are "Enuma Elish," "Enki and Ninhursas," "Atrahasis Epic," and "Enidu Genesis."

[43] Tom Wright. *The Original Jesus: The Life and Vision of a Revolutionary.*

44 The similarities between other Near East texts and Genesis 1–2 are primordial chaos, the mention of rest for the god(s) after creation, the presence of a sacred "tree," and a universal flood (although that is later in Genesis). But make no mistake, Genesis is a bold and world-altering retelling. It is profoundly original—and true.

45 Terrence E. Fretheim. *The Book of Genesis: The New Interpreter's Bible, Volume 1.*

46 Jeremiah 4.23

47 I think someone once told a story about that. Luke 12.15–21.

48 That's interesting—people travelling to another country out of desperation only to be met with suspicion and prejudice.

49 Exodus 1.17

50 Chapters in *God's Story: Reading the Bible as Script and Scripture* by Joshua McNall.

51 As I am sure many of you have noticed, this isn't intended to be a scholarly work. But if it were, this would be the place to discuss the influence of Platonic thinking on the Church. Much of our obsession with leaving comes from a Greek perspective on reality. Even though old Plato cared for things like justice in the present age, many who were influenced by his work did not. From them, the picture emerges of a present world that is an illusion and of a reality that lay outside of space and time. Within such a perspective, the name of the game is getting "there," to reality. Does that sound similar to any presentation of the Gospel that you've heard? Well, that is the influence of Plato, not Jesus.

52 I Thessalonians 4.15–18

53 Philippians 3.20

54 Philippians 3.21

55 Confession: So much of this chapter is inspired by N.T. Wright. My hope one day is to do his laundry. This particular passage comes from an interesting read, *Judas and the Gospel of Jesus.*

56 This discussion about the future moving towards the present is discussed in a book called, *The Return of Jesus in Early Christianity.* By John T. Carroll with Alexandra R. Brown, Claudia J. Setzer, Jeffrey S. Siker.

57 I know a lot of Christians have a real problem with Obama or any Democrat, but the young man who said this was African American. For him, there was a bit deeper significance than left versus right.

58 This frightening statistic was uncovered in my home town, Tulsa, Oklahoma, by the Lewin Group. Here, people who live in poorer parts of the city live fourteen years less than people just blocks away. It's a complex problem, but an unacceptable one nonetheless. Even if you're not from Tulsa, chances are the statistics are similar in your city.

59 I recently heard of a gene discovered in humans that allows some of us to go with less sleep than others. The hope is that by discovering this gene some sort of therapy could be devised that would allow us to go with less sleep so that we could work more. Someone sabotage this project please.

60 Do yourself a favor and read *No Future without Forgiveness* by Desmond Tutu.

61 Sorry Merriam-Webster's. You're helpful most of the time.

62 Is this oversimplified? Yes. Is it untrue? No. On the left, you will find a larger social consciousness. On the right, a larger personal consciousness. Not to be missed is the confusing contradictions within our either-or morality. On one side you can have a deep concern for creation in protecting the environment and caring for the world's poor, and yet have no problem with the taking of pre-natal life. On the other side, there can

be a deep caring for the American unborn, and yet a strange enthusiasm for the dropping of copious bombs on people of other countries. These are a few of the many contradictions that make both camps indefensible.

[63] "The Jesus of Uncool: Chris Martin" (The Rolling Stone Interview). By Brian Hiatt. www.rollingstone.com/news/cover-story/21185368/page/1

[64] Deuteronomy 13.4

[65] This commentary is found in the Talmud. The specific citation is *Sotah* 14a.

[66] Matthew, Mark, and Luke all tell this most famous parable, but only Mark and Luke give the progression I am talking about. Check out Mark 4–5, and Luke 8.1–39.

[67] In no way am I bashing anyone else's interpretation. But often when we hear this parable, we reflect on what it means for us to become good soil. I think that's great. But notice Jesus isn't talking about changing soil types (metaphorically), he is stating a reality to his disciples. Also, Near Eastern people were "dyadic," which means they thought of themselves as a group or collectively. So "soil" would be about "peoples," that is, as a group. So the question is what "group" or "groups" are the good soil?

[68] One of my professors writes extensively on the parables. He is considered an authority. I generously estimate that I agree with about zero percent of his conclusions, but a look at the title should give some understanding to parables as tools to help us see reality differently. *Re-Imagine the World: An Introduction to the Parables of Jesus,* by Bernard Brandon Scott.

[69] The prophet Isaiah compared Israel to a vineyard that failed to grow any substantial harvest. As Isaiah gets a vision of the future, he sees God making a renewed Israel that will produce a proper crop, which is a reference to the future return from

exile. There is good reason to suppose that Jesus is intentionally referencing this idea when he tells this parable. For instance, he quotes Isaiah 6.9–10 as a way of attaching his whole parable to that central vineyard idea. So it is reasonable that Jesus' disciples come to understand Jesus as proclaiming the beginning of God's renewed Israel, the true return from exile. It is worthy to note that Matthew, Mark, and Luke all record Jesus' reference to Isaiah, and John records a reference to the same passage as well (though with no mention of the parable).

[70] This hair-splitting expansion of the Torah was known as "halaka."

[71] N.T. Wright does a great job of expressing this principle in greater detail in his book, *The Challenge of Jesus.*

[72] A scholar named Ben Witherington understands the Parable of the Soils in a similar light. If you get bored, check out: "On the Road with Mary Magdalene, Joanna, Susanna, and the Other Disciples: Luke 8.1–3," found in *A Feminist Companion to Luke* by Amy-Jill Levine.

[73] I must give credit where credit is due. A great friend and emerging scholar, Josh McNall coined this phrase. And I stole it from him.

[74] In Jewish literature, often the "middle" of anything is of huge importance. This form of writing or poetry is called "chiastic construction."

[75] Leviticus 18.8 and 23.22

[76] I got this translation and interpretation from Everett Fox in his work, *The Five Books of Moses.*

[77] James 1.27

[78] Again this comes from Fox.

[79] Sometimes also referred to as Mithras, Mithra was originally an Indo-Iranian deity. The cult that followed him in the Mediterranean was exclusively male and reserved for soldiers and elites. Within the cult was a significant scale of hierarchy. The cult appealed for many reasons, but central to its ethos was a promise for life after death. As the cult progressed, carvings depict Helios/Sol (the sun God) bowing before Mithra, making him the true ruler of the sun.

[80] If you are interested in learning about Mithra's birth for yourself or any other bit of cultural background in the Early Church period, a great place to start is *Exploring the New Testament World: An Illustrated Guide to the World Of Jesus and the First Christians,* by Albert A. Bell.

[81] This is a joke.

[82] Romans 12.21

[83] I first heard this take on Paul's stay in Ephesus from Rob Bell. I would highly recommend his series, "Jesus Wants to Save Christians." You can purchase it on www.marshill.org.

[84] The Temple of Artemis also acted as a primitive banking system. People put their money in the temple treasury, believing Artemis would protect it, and then the priests would loan out the money with interest to others. The whole scheme made Ephesus incredibly wealthy.

[85] Acts 19.35–41

[86] Luke 5

[87] Jeremiah 16.16

[88] Ezekiel 29.3–5

[89] This interpretation was formed with the help of Ben Witherington III in his work, *What Have They Done with Jesus: Beyond Strange Theories and Bad History—Why We Can Trust the Bible.*

90 Actually true. The way you dressed identified you as a member of your community and your status. Thank goodness those days are over. This might be part of the reason Jesus tells a story about a Jew who is beaten and whose clothes are stolen from him. Who will care for this man when it is unclear what group he is part of?

91 I Corinthians 3.9

92 I stole this quote from an Irish youth pastor reflecting on the life of Rich Mullins in a film called, *Homeless Man: The Restless Heart of Rich Mullins.* You should watch it.

93 One of my personal heroes who I hope to meet someday, St. Ignatius of Antioch. He wrote these words while awaiting his execution for being a Christian, in his letter to the Romans, chapter 3.

94 I John 4.12

95 Ephesians 5.22–33

96 Genesis 2.15

97 Genesis 2.18

98 Genesis 2.20

99 Genesis 2.23

100 This chapter is about more than the institution of marriage, it's about our partnership with God. So what I am saying in reference to marriage can be understood also in relation to God. But we can't have sex with God. Maybe a parallel for sex is worship. Notice how the Anglican marriage vow states, "with my body, I thee worship." If we'd say a marriage with sex but no larger vision is in trouble, could we say the same thing about a spirituality that has worship but no mission?

101 At the close of Jesus' most prolific speech about what it means to be part of his revolution, he says, "Therefore everyone who

hears these words of mine and puts them into practice is like a wise man who built his house on the rock" (Matt. 7.24–25).

When Jesus was looking to compare his life and instruction to something concrete, he picks a foundation? Well, yes. A foundation, after all, is just the beginning. It's useless unless it becomes something more. Jesus is plugged into the original idea that partnership between the divine and human is the way the world works.

As Paul said, "By the grace God has given me, I laid a foundation as an expert builder, and someone else is building on it. But each one should be careful how he builds. For no one can lay any foundation other than the one already laid, which is Jesus Christ" (I Cor. 3.10–11).

Jesus is the beginning. He is like a foundation. Someone else has to build. Once again, the writers of the Bible show God and his plan in need of human partnership. The point isn't simply to look at the foundation and admire its size and shape. The point is to see it, study it, and then get to work.

God wants certain things to happen in his world. Those things come to reality through people partnering with him.

102 II Corinthians 1.5

103 Saul of course is a Jewish name. A lot of people think he gave up his name and his Jewish-ness as well. But Saul was to take the Jewish Jesus to a non-Jewish world. The name change to Paul was more about communicating this vocation than about leaving his Jewish heritage behind.

104 Acts 9.15–16

105 Isaiah 53.4–5. Just read the whole chapter.

106 This is really a universal understanding. But for an interesting read that includes the concept of *shalom,* check out, *Jesus the Jewish Theologian* by Brad H. Young.

107 Maybe Jesus knew that the victim often becomes the oppressor, and he just wanted to put a stop to it all together. For a great discussion on this topic check out, *Exclusion and Embrace: A Theological Exploration of Identity, Otherness, and Reconciliation* by Miroslav Volf.

108 I think the phrase "shalom of God" is a frequent Rob Bell-ism. His minimalist style has been hugely influential and I appreciate much of what he has to say.

109 Luke 6.20

110 Interestingly, Jesus turned over the tables in the Temple, which was run by corrupt officials known as Sadducees. They were getting rich off the sacrificial system and by living in Rome's back pocket. But when Jesus protests at the Temple grounds, he calls it a den of "thieves." It's a quote from Jeremiah, but the Greek word for thieves is *"lestes,"* which can be translated as brigand or revolutionary. Jesus is also warning against the movement launched by the Pharisees and their hot-headed cousins, the Zealots. Because of its symbolic significance, a few years later, the Temple Mount was a major staging area and headquarters for a revolution. It failed. So in one move, Jesus calls out both movements and both methods of partnering with God.

111 Matthew 5.44

112 Matthew 26.26

113 Matthew 26.28

114 Colossians 1.20 with some interpretive help from Andrew Lincoln, *The Letter to the Colossians: New Interpreter's Bible Commentary, Volume XI.*

115 Colossians 1.15

116 John 20.21

117 Read any Hebrew prophet and you'll see it. If you don't see it, read anything by Walter Bruggeman.

118 Isaiah 2.4

119 Don't worry. Patrick is getting his well.

120 Romans 8.22

121 Romans 8.23

122 N.T Wright, Marcus Borg. *The Meaning of Jesus: Two Visions.*

123 It is interesting to parallel Paul's use of labor as a metaphor. In Romans 8, creation, Christians and God groan together as we wait and work for the repaired world. In I Thessalonians 5.3, Paul says that those who believe in the Roman propaganda slogan of "peace and security" "will not escape." It's as if Paul is saying the world birthed through the suffering love of the Messiah is sure to come (Rom. 8.28–39), while the world birthed through the violence of the sword will be stillborn.

124 I would highly suggest the book, *The Poor Will Be Glad: Joining the Revolution to Lift the World out of Poverty* by Peter Greer and Phil Smith. It gives wise guidance on what this sort of lifestyle could actually look like.

125 Found in Luke 24.13–35.

126 Reported by the Lewin Group.